Called into Communion

Called into Communion

A Paradigm Shift in Holiness Theology

By Susan B. Carole

PICKWICK *Publications* · Eugene, Oregon

CALLED INTO COMMUNION
A Paradigm Shift in Holiness Theology

Pickwick Publications
An Imprint of Wipf and Stock Publishers
199 W. 8th Ave., Suite 3
Eugene, OR 97401

www.wipfandstock.com

ISBN 13: 978-1-61097-965-8

Cataloguing-in-Publication data:

Carole, Susan B.

Called into communion : a paradigm shift in holiness theology / Susan B. Carole, with a foreword by Richard B. Steele.

xiv + 118 pp. ; 23 cm. Includes bibliographical references.

ISBN 13: 978-1-61097-965-8

1. Wesley, John, 1703–1791. 2. Holiness—Christianity. 3. Holiness churches—Doctrines. I. Steele, Richard B., 1952–. II. Title.

BT767 C176 2013

Manufactured in the U.S.A.

To Georges
Nadine
Rémy
Pascal
With gratitude and very much love

Contents

Foreword

SUSAN CAROLE HAS GIVEN us a book that is both courageous and constructive. She displays a comprehensive grasp of the development of theological anthropology and moral psychology within the Wesleyan-Holiness tradition, and traces the gradual shift that took place within the tradition during the nineteenth and twentieth centuries away from the theocentrism of the founders toward the anthropocentrism and moralism so widespread today. She shows how the original Wesleyan doctrines of "free grace" and "salvation by faith" were slowly but steadily replaced by a synergistic account of Christian experience and praxis that underestimates the severity of human sin, overestimates the human capacity to conquer it, and trivializes what a truly sanctified life would look like. Carole thus does for American Methodism something akin to what Joseph Haroutunian did for American Calvinism eighty years ago in *Piety versus Moralism*, and her contribution to Wesleyan self-understanding is long overdue and much needed. This book is, as I say, a courageous performance for a young scholar, for she unhesitatingly exposes the subtle theological miscues of such patriarchs and matriarchs of the tradition as Phoebe Palmer, H. Ray Dunning, and Mildred Wynkoop, though she does so in a gracious and respectful tone, giving credit where credit is due for new insights and legitimate developments. This is critique without caricature, reminiscent of John Wesley's own manner of engaging in religious dispute.

But Carole's work is constructive, too. For she attempts to rehabilitate the hallmark doctrines of the Wesleyan-Holiness tradition by affirming the power of the Holy Spirit to transform the hearts and lives of those who, through faith, enter into communion with Jesus Christ, and who, through self-giving love, enter into communion with each other. She skillfully demonstrates that there is need in the Christian life both for decisive "crisis" moments and for sustained "progress" through the assiduous practice of the works of piety and mercy, and through diligent participation in the fellowship and corporate discipline of the church. Indeed, the very fact that a fierce and protracted dispute has gone on within the movement between those who insist that sanctification is an instantaneous experience and those who regard it as the natural result of religious maturation is a sign of our pervasive failure to understand Christian experience in rigorously and consistently *theological* terms, that is, as the result of the operation of divine grace upon and within the souls of fellowshipping believers. All too often Wesleyans have interpreted the life of faith in predominantly *psychological* or *ethical* terms. They have seen it as a series of emotionally cataclysmic events that believers feel they "must" undergo, or as a predetermined sequence of developmental stages through which they "will" automatically pass, or as a string of onerous obligations and white-knuckled self-denials. But when the *ordo salutis* is reduced to a punch list of do's and don'ts or a flow chart of predictable spiritual episodes or stages, the result is "zeal without knowledge" in one of its many forms—obsessive spiritual pulse-taking, complacent spiritual navel-gazing, hysterical revivalism, quietistic do-nothingism, hypocritical pharisaism, grim dutifulness, dogmatic quarrelsomeness and so forth. All of these aberrations are well-documented in the Wesleyan-Holiness tradition, and Carole shows that they are consequences of a severely defective picture of divine-human interaction. She does not deny the descriptive power of psychological accounts of religious experience or the need for normative ethical prescription: these have their rightful place in her scheme. Things go wrong, however, when accounts of Christian experience and praxis overlook or downplay the divine initiative: psychological and ethical reductionism inevitably leads to religious self-deception and pastoral manipulation. The only safeguard is a robust account of the way God's sovereign grace instigates and guides human transformation, not abridging our freedom and thereby attenuating our moral accountability, but rather breaking the power of our inbred sin and capacitating us for joyous worship, righteous action, and loving spontaneity.

Carole's theological anthropology is thus marked by a series of polarities held in dynamic tension. In her doctrine of salvation, she balances justification against sanctification: the former denotes the change which faith in Christ's sacrifice for our sins works in our *relationship* with the Father, while the latter denotes the change which faith works in *ourselves*, as the Spirit relentlessly purifies our intentions, corrects our habituated idolatries, strengthens our holy commitments, nurtures our virtues, and propels us steadily toward Christian perfection. In her description of religious experience, she balances instantaneity and gradualism, recognizing the key role played by moments of critical decision as well as our need for long stretches of quiet, regulated growth. In her account of Christian discipline, she balances the works of piety against the works of mercy, showing how piety keeps the works of mercy godly, while mercy keeps the works of piety humane. In her rendering of Christian subjectivity, she balances the "inward" against the "outward," taking gracious affections and holy tempers as action-motivating dispositions (not just emotional episodes), and taking righteous conduct as responsiveness to the indwelling Spirit (not just as dutiful behavior).

This is an inspiring vision of Christian experience and praxis, one that is deeply rooted in the Wesleyan Holiness heritage and immensely relevant to the cultural realities and missional challenges of our time. It is my honor and pleasure to commend it to your consideration.

Richard B. Steele
Professor of Moral & Historical Theology
Seattle Pacific University

Acknowledgments

I am glad for this opportunity to publicly express my heartfelt appreciation to the many people who have contributed to this book, and without whom its completion would not have been possible. As such, *Called into Communion* represents the encouragement, prayers, and thoughts of the body of believers, rather than the single writer to whom authorship is ascribed. Beyond the persons mentioned herein, there are many others who have contributed to my personal journey with God the Father, through the grace of our Lord Jesus Christ, by the Spirit of Truth. This book is an expression of that journey—a day by day participation in the fellowship of Holy Love.

I thank my family for their faith, encouragement, and continual prayers. My husband, Georges, freed me from numerous obligations so that I would have time to write. His confidence that I would write well has helped me to persevere to the end. My children, Nadine, Rémy, and Pascal knew the words to sympathize with my frustrations and encourage me to believe that God would never cease to strengthen and guide my endeavor. The faith of my brothers and sisters that I would excel motivated me to do my best. Thank you for believing. Thank you for praying.

The wonderful community of believers at Calvin Theological Seminary has shaped me in the requisite disciplines and graces requisite of a theologian who might be useful to the church of Jesus Christ in some small measure. They gave me tools for right reflection, excellence and clarity. Moreover, they have instilled in me the importance of and desire for piety and godly character by their own example. Special mention must be made of Ronald Feenstra, who has patiently pressed me into precise reflection and a stance of humility before Scripture and Christian tradition. In addition, I am grateful to John Cooper, Lee Hardy, and Richard Muller for helping me connect the theological and philosophical strands

Acknowledgments

of Christian tradition to the contemporary theological and ecclesial landscape. Thank you all for the gift of theology, this joyful science.

Beyond this, mention must be made of my friends and colleagues in the Church of the Nazarene. I thank the Michigan District Superintendent, John Seaman, and all the members of the district who have prayed for me and listened to me talk about my work. Their keen interest in my research continues to be an encouragement. I am grateful also for the support of fellow Nazarene scholars Mark Maddix of Northwest Nazarene University, Ron Benefiel of Point Loma Nazarene University, and Roger Hahn of Nazarene Theological Seminary for their endorsement of my work.

In the collegiality of the Wesleyan Theological Society, I have found champions of high caliber. I thank Richard Steele of Seattle Pacific University for writing the foreword and Ken Collins of Asbury Theological Seminary for his endorsement. The dialogue I am privileged to enjoy with these fine theologians continues to be a source of enrichment.

I am thankful to Pickwick Publications for publishing this work and to editors Christian Amondson and Robin Parry for helping me with the publication process.

I especially thank my readers for taking the time to consider this articulation of what it means that God is Holy Love. I pray that something in these pages will ignite and nurture your passion for God, whose mercy has no edge.

Susan B. Carole
Michigan
October 2012

1

The Need for a Paradigm Shift
in Holiness Theology

THE HISTORIC MISSION AND self-understanding of the Wesleyan-Holiness tradition is inseparable from holiness theology, the tradition's distinctive teaching. Holiness theology is primarily concerned with the doctrine of entire sanctification, understood as a post-justification cleansing from inbred sin by the Holy Spirit. The experiential nature of holiness theology carries a latent tendency to subjectivism, which obscures the implications of the teaching beyond the subjective locus. Since the holiness message is one of freedom from self-involvement, a self-referential articulation introduces an element of incoherence in theological construal. The project undertaken in this book is to develop a theocentric and experiential holiness theology by considering the teaching in terms of its transcendent goal, participation in God. On this view, holiness theology finds its root and possibility in the triune life of holy love.

There are indications of a need for renewal in holiness theology. In 2004, scholars and denominational leaders gathered for the Wesleyan Holiness Study Project, an enquiry into the identity of the tradition and its mission in the twenty-first century.[1] The Project recognized the need for revitalization of ecclesial life and concluded that, to this end, a compelling articulation of the holiness message was essential.[2] It acknowledged that the church needs a unifying and powerful message grounded in the holiness of God. Without such a message, leaders have no single determinative vision for ecclesial life: "they have no compelling message

1. Mannoia and Thorsen, *Holiness Manifesto.*
2. Ibid., 18.

1

to give, no compelling vision of God, no transformational understanding of God's otherness. They know it and long to find the centering power of a message that makes a difference. Now more than ever, they long to soak up a deep understanding of God's call to holiness—transformed living."[3] Congregations crave genuine unity in Christ: "they want to see the awesomeness of God's holiness that compels us to oneness in which there is a testimony of power."[4] The Project calls the tradition to renewed emphasis on holiness, which is "the heart of Scripture concerning Christian existence for all times—and clearly for our time."[5] The conclusion reached by the Wesleyan Holiness Study Project is that the holiness message should be the compelling center of ecclesial life.

A single compelling articulation of holiness theology seems to be wanting. Currently, there are at least two interpretations of entire sanctification—instantaneous perfection and progressive sanctification.[6] The former position affirms entire sanctification as an instantaneous, post-justification experience, while the latter favors a gradual process of perfectioning in love. Thus, there stands at present a "crisis" view and a "process" view of entire sanctification. The coexistence of two disparate positions has undermined the vitality of holiness doctrine. The immediate theological situation is that there is no single understanding of holiness theology that can form a locus of consensus within the Wesleyan-Holiness tradition.

I suggest that the present impasse points to an underlying problem of theological approach. A self-referential approach has compromised the sustainability of holiness teaching because it overshadows grace and limits the significance of holiness theology to its subjective dimension. The approach to the crisis-process question is itself an indication of subjectivism. For example, one challenge to the crisis view is that instantaneity relates to the *form* of personal experience, rather than to the theological *content* of the teaching.[7] This indicates an approach to the problem from an experiential rather than theological perspective.

---

3. Ibid., 18–19.

4. Ibid., 19.

5. Ibid., 19.

6. Christensen, "*Theosis* and Sanctification," 219

7. For example, Dunning claims that the crisis view is due to the influence of nineteenth century revivalism, and as such, is neither necessary nor desirable in holiness theology (Dunning, "Towards a New Paradigm," 154).

There are other indications of subjectivism and its related concerns in holiness theology. In some theological accounts, becoming holy is the presupposed goal of entire sanctification.[8] The teaching urges believers to seek the experience in view of empowerment for a life of holiness and service.[9] Limiting the aim of the experience to personal spirituality pre-empts unequivocal grounding of human holiness in the holiness of God. The principal content of such theologies is the believer's role in obtaining the experience. When such accounts do not also underscore the role of the Holy Spirit, human agency inadvertently obtains undue importance.[10] Giving primary consideration to personal spirituality restricts holiness theology to the sphere of ethics.[11] This limitation hinders consideration of the full ecclesial import of holiness theology beyond individual experience. Most importantly, the underlying problem posed by a self-referential approach is the introduction of an internal contradiction in holiness theology itself: while holiness theology attests to liberation from self-orientation, a self-referential approach seems to foster undue self-appraisal.

This analysis of the problem suggests that the task is to break out of the self-referential paradigm without undermining the importance of the life of holiness and individual moral responsibility. This book develops holiness theology in terms of its transcendent goal, fullness of communion with God. I define fullness of communion as the divine-human relation of mutual self-giving in which the believer is fully responsive to divine lordship and love. This relationship requires the experience of entire sanctification and effects moral transformation. This perspective extends the horizon of reflection to the Wesleyan *ordo salutis* as the necessary locus of the experience, and the divine life of holy love as its necessary ground. Moral responsibility is an imperative of grace. Holiness theology, understood in terms of communion, can function as the underwriting theological principle for ecclesial life. Subsequent chapters demonstrate the pertinence of the proposed approach and elaborate the dynamics and ecclesial significance of holiness theology.

Chapter 2 accounts for the existence of the subjective strand in holiness teaching at the present time. Wesley's experiential soteriology collapsed into a self-referential paradigm through its modification during

8. Taylor, *Theological Formulation*, 158–59.

9. Grider, *Wesleyan-Holiness Theology*, 367.

10. Ibid., 367–455.

11. Wiley, *Christian Theology*, 3: 7–100; Dunning, *Grace, Faith and Holiness*, 498–99.

the nineteenth-century Holiness Movement. The Movement propagated entire sanctification as a crisis experience in abstraction from its theological context and with a concept of faith that emphasized human agency. The confluence of these theological modifications in the context of nineteenth-century revivalism produced an anthropocentric holiness teaching. This chapter traces these developments and shows that, in spite of theological endeavors in the twentieth century, holiness theology continues to evidence a strand of subjectivism.

Chapter 3 develops the communion paradigm with faith as its core principle and participation in God as its point of reference. This is an appropriate approach because participation in God is a fundamental and common theme in both strands of holiness thought and is a corollary of the Wesleyan conception of faith. Moreover, the goal of entire sanctification is full relationality in the divine-human interaction. This approach produces a conceptual framework that orients holiness theology to its root in the holy love of God and dissolves the self-referential paradigm.

Chapter 4 explicates entire sanctification within the communion paradigm. Communion with God begins at justification and deepens in the matrix of divine-human reciprocity. Entire sanctification is a decisive moment of faith in which the Holy Spirit cleanses away inherited sin through the revelation and impartation of divine holiness and love. Inherited sin is a pervasive principle of unbelief and idolatry. Freedom from inherited sin allows more receptivity to the Holy Spirit. The fullness of the Spirit is the cause of the believer's wholehearted love for God and allegiance to His lordship. Thus, through entire sanctification, the Holy Spirit draws the believer into fullness of communion. The rationale for holiness theology is that fullness of communion is a divine command and promise, and that entire sanctification is the threshold of fullness of communion.

Chapter 5 discusses the ecclesial significance of holiness theology. Holiness theology, articulated in terms of participation in God, can function as the underwriting theological principle of ecclesial culture and mission. When, through the means of grace, ecclesial life orients to communion with God, the church develops doxological corporate character. Although undertaken through diverse forms, the quest for the knowledge of God transcends traditions. This shared quest can strengthen the connection between the Wesleyan-Holiness and other theological traditions. A Christian community oriented to fullness of communion derives its missional rationale from its passion for the divine mission. Participation in God includes participation in His vision and His mission. Fullness of communion allows for deeper engagement in God's passion for the other so that the church incarnates grace by becoming a means of grace.

Chapter 6 summarizes the aspects of the communion paradigm that free holiness theology from subjectivism. The fundamental contribution of this project is that it seeks to develop a theological method for holiness theology that is theocentric and experiential, rather than anthropocentric. Thinking past personal sanctification and into the divine life discloses divine holiness as the cause of fellowship with God and the guarantee of human holiness. Holiness is the consequence of a relationship that thrives through the exercise of faith in the sphere of grace. In sum, viewing the *ordo salutis* in terms of communion with God illuminates the connection of holiness theology to systematic theology as a whole and diffuses the perception of holiness theology as a mere idiosyncrasy of the Wesleyan-Holiness tradition, or a relic of nineteenth-century revivalism.

2

From Experiential to Self-Referential Holiness Theology

Introduction

The previous chapter identified a strand of subjectivism in holiness theology and pointed to its related concerns. The present chapter briefly traces the trajectory of holiness theology from Wesley's Christian perfection to the present. This overview indicates that holiness theology shifted from Wesley's experiential conception to a self-referential focus during the nineteenth-century Holiness Movement. Wesley's concept of faith led to a dynamic and experiential view of Christian perfection. However, the nineteenth-century teaching of entire sanctification included a volitional view of faith and a correspondence of the experience with pentecostal baptism with the Holy Spirit. These were some of the changes that introduced a subjective orientation into holiness theology. The twentieth century saw creative revisions aimed at harmonizing both strands of the received tradition. Nonetheless, subjectivism continues to linger in some explications of entire sanctification.

Heart Religion: Wesley's Experiential Theology

To begin with, I wish to show that Wesley construes Christian perfection within a dynamic *ordo salutis*. The experiential nature of Wesley's thought comes to light in the relation between faith and heart religion. Faith is a divine gift that brings personal conviction of spiritual truth.

Heart religion refers to the ongoing transformation of the disposition of the heart through the Holy Spirit. Wesley's conception of the faith-heart religion relation produces an experiential *ordo salutis* that advances by growing faith and increasing transformation. Christian perfection arises within this soteriological framework as the culmination of heart religion through the threshold experience of entire sanctification. As this section demonstrates, for Wesley, theological truth must translate into the way one lives. His consistent assertion is that the victory over sin accomplished *for* humanity in Christ must be actualized *in* the hearts of individuals through the Holy Spirit. Christian perfection is an outcome of this experiential matrix.

Faith

Faith is personal appropriation of the knowledge of God. It is a divine gift that imparts spiritual sight and spiritual light.[1] Spiritual sight is the capacity to apprehend spiritual knowledge. Spiritual light is experiential knowledge of God.[2] Thus, saving faith is conviction that the reconciling work of Christ was accomplished on one's personal behalf.[3] Faith, then, is personally meaningful and transformative knowledge, a complex of intellectual assent, trust, and personal experience.[4] Intellectual assent is adherence to a particular belief system. Trust is lively confidence that the knowledge given is truth. Personal experience is the mode of knowing in which truth obtains existential significance. The baseline of this faith-complex is personal experience. One's chosen belief system forms a cognitive framework for personal experience of God, which includes

1. "Scripture Way," *Works* VI: 46–47. Wesley argues that since ideas come to us through our senses, we need spiritual senses to discern spiritual reality ("Earnest Appeal," *Works* VIII: 13). Several scholars agree that Wesley's idea of spiritual senses reflects the empiricism of John Locke (See for example, Brantley, *Locke, Wesley, English Romanticism*; Dreyer, "Faith and Experience"; Thobaben, "Holy Knowing"; Wood, "Wesley's Epistemology"; Wesley himself expresses agreement with Locke's principal tenet that there are no innate ideas ("Mr. Locke's *Essay*," *Works* XIII: 455–56).

2. "Discoveries of Faith," *Works* VII: 232.

3. "Scripture Way," *Works* VI: 46.

4. "Salvation by Faith," *Works* V: 9. Matthews argues that Wesley's view of faith is a complex of "*fides, fiducia*, and *feeling*." *Fides* refers to intellectual assent, *fiducia* to trust, and *feeling*, to spiritual experience of God. He concludes that for Wesley, "the *particular* understanding of faith as one's personal spiritual experience of God's grace and mercy" is foundational to *fiducia* and *fides* (Matthews, "'With the Eyes of Faith,'" 414).

the dimension of trust-response. This interaction of divine self-revelation and human appropriation explains the *ordo salutis* as a movement from faith to faith. The gift of faith is to be distinguished from the exercise of faith as a human response. Acting upon the knowledge of faith opens up the way for more knowledge.[5]

Heart Religion

Heart religion refers to the transformative impact of the personal knowledge of God that comes by faith.[6] Through obedient response to the Holy Spirit, one's disposition takes on the attitudes of love. Transformed disposition produces virtue and happiness.[7] Inward maturity produces outward transformation. New attitudes lead to more fruitful relationships since there is an increasing capacity to approach others with mercy, faith, hope and love.[8] For Wesley, this transformation is true religion or the religion of the heart. Although Wesley insists on both inward and outward transformation, the basis for change is the believer's personal relationship with God. To conclude, Wesley's experiential vision avoids subjectivism because it is based on a concept of faith as divine gift, of which transformation is a product.

---

5. "Discoveries of Faith," *Works* VII: 236–37 (Wesley distinguishes three degrees of faith—the faith of a servant, the faith of a son, and the faith of a father. The faith of a servant is belief in God and desire to obey His commandments. The faith of a son or saving faith is personal knowledge of the love of God in Jesus Christ. Saving faith marks the beginning of new life in Christ and continues to increase under the tutelage of the Holy Spirit through the means of grace. The faith of a father refers to mature faith that ensues in wholehearted love for God and neighbor. Mature faith does not refer to a static end-point. On the contrary, Wesley urges mature believers to grow in faith and love.).

6. Collins shows that "heart" in the Wesley corpus refers to dispositions, tempers and affections. The transforming power of the Holy Spirit progressively shapes the heart in love and holiness. Dispositions and tempers are enduring and inherent qualities of a person. Affections are expressions of the will, or expressions of dispositions and tempers (Collins, "Wesley's Topography," 162–75). Similarly, Maddox describes Wesley's "heart" as "inner motivating inclinations." Maddox remarks that heart religion indicates the importance of the inward inclinations (dispositions, tempers and affections) for outward moral activity (Maddox, "Change of Affections," 16).

7. "Earnest Appeal," *Works* VII: 4.

8. "Farther Appeal," *Works* VIII: 244.

Christian Perfection

Christian perfection arises from and reflects Wesley's experiential and teleological hermeneutic.[9] It is heart religion in its fullest sense, both as a culmination and an ongoing process. Christian perfection comes through the crisis experience of entire sanctification, which arises in the matrix of the salvific process. In sum, Wesley's teaching constitutes a balance of crisic and gradual elements, which together produce a soteriological framework shaped by the principle of heart religion.

Christian perfection is the culmination of heart religion.[10] It is wholehearted love for God and one's neighbor. God is the desire of the heart and the source of happiness.[11] The outflow of love for God is love for one's neighbor.[12] Love for God purifies the heart from sinful dispositions. The believer obeys God because the heart's whole desire is to please God.[13] The basis of wholehearted love is transformative faith, which purifies the heart and fills it with love.[14] The correspondence between the description of Christian perfection and mature faith shows that Christian perfection is the full actualization of heart religion.

While Christian perfection is the goal of heart religion, those perfected in love continue from faith to faith.[15] In fact, perfection suggests growing in love. Schlimm remarks that for Wesley, wholehearted love can grow in intensity and in resemblance to God's love.[16] In addition, purity of intent does not always translate into perfection in behavior. Christian perfection does not include perfect knowledge or understanding. Those perfected in love continue to live with "a thousand nameless defects,

---

9. Wesley's teaching on Christian perfection remains consistent from 1740 onwards and can be understood primarily by way of "A Plain Account of Christian Perfection" (Smith, "Wesley and the Second Blessing;" "Chronological List"). Several of Wesley's sermons also treat Christian perfection, for example, "On Perfection," *Works* VI: 411–24, "Scripture Way," *Works* VI: 43–54, "Discoveries of Faith," *Works* VII: 231–38. See Noble ("John Wesley as a Theologian") for an overview of major works concerning Wesley's doctrine of Christian perfection.

10. Christian perfection is the goal of heart religion, since Christian perfection means that love is the single inward inclination (Maddox, "Change of Affections," 21).

11. "Plain Account," *Works* XI: 371.

12. Ibid., 372.

13. Ibid., 372.

14. "Almost Christian," *Works* V: 21–23.

15. "Discoveries of Faith," *Works* VII: 236–37.

16. Schlimm, "Growth in Wesley's Doctrine of Perfection," 133.

either in conversation or behavior."[17] Ignorance, bodily weaknesses, and personality traits are some of the factors that may hinder the free expression of love in one's attitudes, words, and actions.[18] Maturity in perfect love means increasing alignment between a heart of perfect love and clarity in expressing love. Accordingly, the concept of Christian perfection includes both a culminating and a processive aspect.

Christian perfection is deliverance from all sin through entire sanctification.[19] Thus, Wesley speaks of "the circumcision of the heart from all filthiness, all inward as well as outward pollution."[20] From the moment of justification, the believer has power over both inward and outward sin.[21] Nonetheless, the carnal mind remains subsequent to justification and is evidenced by one's proneness to evil. While the carnal mind does not forfeit the favor of God, the believer is called to resist its inclinations through the help of the Holy Spirit.[22] Gradual sanctification brings increasing awareness of the carnal mind and the need for deliverance, culminating in entire sanctification, the moment of deliverance. Entire sanctification

17 "Plain Account," *Works* XI: 374.

18. Wesley refers to three types of imperfections that are consistent with Christian perfection. First, imperfection in knowledge; second, susceptibility to temptation; third, infirmity, or "weakness or slowness of understanding, irregular quickness or heaviness of imagination." These infirmities may be considered personality traits in the sense that they refer to a person's characteristic responses to situations and other persons ("Plain Account," *Works* XI: 374).

19. "Christian perfection" refers to the state of loving God wholeheartedly. "Entire sanctification" refers to the crisis experience in which the Holy Spirit delivers the believer from all sin and ushers in the state of Christian perfection. This distinction is not consistently held in Wesley's thought. For example, in "Plain Account," Wesley refers to the instantaneous experience of cleansing from sin as "entire sanctification" (*Works* XI: 389). In the same treatise, he describes Christian perfection as an instantaneous experience (*Works* XI: 393). Thus, Wesley seems to use these terms interchangeably.

20. "Plain Account," *Works* XI: 444.

21. "Sin in Believers," *Works* V: 147.

22. Ibid., 155–56. In "Justification by Faith," Wesley distinguishes between justification and initial sanctification. Sanctification is being made actually just and righteous. It is "in some degree, the immediate fruit of justification, but, nevertheless, is a distinct gift of God, and of a totally different nature. The one [justification] implies what God does for us through his Son; the other, what he works in us by his Spirit" (*Works* V: 56). Justification is "the clearing . . . from the accusation brought against us by the law . . . whereas we have transgressed the law of God, and thereby deserved the damnation of hell, God does not inflict on those who are justified the punishment which they had deserved" (*Works* V: 56). Justification does not mean that God considers the unrighteous to be righteous. Instead, it is the forgiveness of sins. Thus, "to him that is justified or forgiven, God 'will not impute sin' to his condemnation" (*Works* V: 57).

is by faith, which, in this case, is the conviction of God's actual, immediate sanctifying work. Thus, for Wesley, entire sanctification is instantaneous because it is by faith. Nevertheless, since it is possible for one to be unaware of the instant of occurrence, the experience may appear to be gradual.[23] A believer may subsequently become aware of having been entirely sanctified by observing a variety of inward and outward changes.

Although it is sometimes claimed that Wesley emphasizes the process over the crisis elements of his soteriology,[24] in fact, crisis plays the crucial role of culminating as well as initializing process. First, crisis is a culmination of the faith process in Wesley's *ordo salutis*. Without the crisis, the process remains incomplete, since the goal of the process is to bring the believer to a crisis point in faith. Furthermore, process, in Wesley's soteriology, tends towards a crisis that ushers in possibilities "that did not previously exist and are not the result of preexisting factors."[25] Collins points out that crisis in Wesley's thought "highlights the utter graciousness" of the gift of salvation as "the work of God *alone*."[26] Second, process is the context of crisis. It is movement towards a goal, whether justification or entire sanctification.[27] In both crises, there is a progressive increase in the knowledge of God, culminating in saving and sanctifying faith respectively.

The teaching of deliverance from inbred sin in this life did not go unopposed in Wesley's milieu.[28] His principal scriptural ground for Christian perfection is that divine promises and commands of love and holiness inhere Scripture.[29] In "On Perfection" he shows that holiness is

23. "Scripture Way," *Works* VI: 53–54.

24. Thus, for example, Maddox states that "while the affirmation of the possibility of entire sanctification may have been *distinctive* of Wesley, the conception of sanctification (as a whole) as the progressive journey in responsive cooperation with God's empowering grace was most *characteristic* of Wesley"(Maddox, *Responsible Grace,*190).

25. Knight , "Love and Freedom ," 63.

26. Collins, *Holy Love*, 16.

27. "Bondage and Adoption," *Works* V: 101–6; Repentance of Believers," *Works* V: 168–70.

28. Cox shows that Wesley's point of division with Calvinism regarding sanctification was that "the believer could be sanctified wholly, or saved from all sin, before the article of death (Cox, *Concept of Perfection*, 111). See also, McGonigle (*Sufficient Saving Grace*, 260–61) for a more detailed treatment of the issues at stake in the Calvinistic opposition to Wesley's teaching in the mid-eighteenth century.

29. Turner argues that "the most significant as well as the most concise exhibition of the Methodist use of Scripture to support the doctrine of sanctification is found in the Annual Minutes, from the year 1744 on" (Turner, *Vision which Transforms*, 242). In the Conference of 1747 the following question is addressed: "Is there any clear

an imperative in both the Old and New Testaments. He reads the great commandment as a promise of deliverance from the carnal mind. He argues that there is a "general and unlimited promise" of inward fulfillment of the great commandment throughout the gospel dispensation, expressed in texts such as "I will put my law in their minds and write them on their hearts." Commands such as "let this mind be in you which was also in Christ Jesus," and "love thy neighbor as thyself," are promises expressed as commands because God "will work in us what he requires of us."[30] The plain sense of Scripture is that God requires and enables human holiness. Both promise and command are for this life since God can sanctify the soul while it is in the body.[31]

In conclusion, entire sanctification is best understood in the context of the soteriological crisis-process relation as the threshold experience that ushers in Christian perfection. Heart religion culminates in Christian perfection. Nonetheless, this stage is itself an ongoing application of wholehearted love to all spheres of life. Thus, Christian perfection is itself a transformative process into which the believer enters

---

scriptural promise . . . that God will save us from all sin?" The response includes both Old and New Testament texts. In the Old Testament the promise of cleansing (Ezek 36:25, 29) and the promise of circumcision of the heart (Deut 30:6) are clear promises of deliverance from all sin. In the New Testament, 1 John 3:8 states that the Son of God was manifested to destroy the works of the devil. This is understood as "the works of the devil, without any limitation or restriction: But all sin is the work of the devil." Furthermore, Christ has given Himself to make the church holy (Eph 5:27). Added to these are the prayers and commands of the New Testament "which are equivalent to the strongest assertions." Prayers referenced in this regard are that of Jesus, "I in them, and thou in me, that they may be made perfect in one" (John 17:23); St. Paul, "that you might be filled with all the fullness of God" (Eph 3:19) and "the very God of peace sanctify you wholly" (1 Thess 5:23). The commands to be perfect (Matt 5:48) and to love God with all the heart, soul and mind (Matt 22:37) indicate that sin should not remain in the heart ("Minutes," *Works* VIII: 294–95). Turner summarizes Wesley's views: Entire sanctification is possible in this life on the basis of the New Testament teaching that 1.) Deliverance is possible (2 Cor. 7:1; 1 Thess 5:23) and 2.) Christians are called to be like God in holiness and love (Matt 5:48; John 17:17–21; 1 Pet 1:15). Regarding the secondness of the experience, the New Testament teaches: 1.) The distinction between sins and inherited sin; 2.) The requirement for cleansing from all sin; 3.) The assurance that those who seek after righteousness will be filled (Turner, *Vision which Transforms*, 256–58). Turner concludes that "in making Christian perfection simply pure love to God and man, Wesley embraced in his teaching the essential message and main trend of both Old and New Testaments" (ibid., 247).

30. "On Perfection," *Works* VI: 411–24.

31. Ibid., 418.

through the experience of entire sanctification, a threshold experience within the salvific process.

Entire Sanctification: The Paradigm Shift of the Holiness Movement

Wesley's Christian perfection obtained particular emphases as it was propagated by other Methodist leaders, which later influenced the shape of holiness teaching in the nineteenth-century Holiness Movement. The Movement arose partly in response to a tendency to a gradualist teaching of Christian perfection as well as a seeming disinterest in the teaching within American Methodism. It aimed at asserting the significance of the crisis experience of entire sanctification. In the context of revivalism, holiness teaching developed an element of urgency. It was understood as the pinnacle of salvation, thereby eclipsing the importance of justification and progressive sanctification. Entire sanctification was correlated with pentecostal baptism, which was understood as a means to spiritual empowerment. The concept of faith carried a strong element of human free will. As a result, holiness teaching became a quest for an experience of personal empowerment by a risk-free, accessible method. The character of the experience as a work of grace was presupposed rather than explicated. Thus, the teaching shifted from an experiential to a self-referential paradigm.

Background Considerations

This section identifies three issues that laid the foundation for the nineteenth-century approach to holiness theology. The teaching of Christian perfection in American Methodism reflected the changes introduced by prominent advocates in British Methodism. A perceived disinterest in teaching Christian perfection within American Methodism led to the advocacy of holiness by prominent Methodists. As holiness teaching crossed denominational lines, it was absorbed into revivalism and took shape within this context. These considerations show the foundational influences that contributed to the subjectivism with which holiness teaching was thenceforth characterized.

The teaching of Christian perfection of the nineteenth-century Holiness Movement reflected the influences of prominent Methodist advocates: John Fletcher (1729–85), Richard Watson (1781–1833), and Adam

Clarke (1760–1832).[32] Fletcher emphasizes the role of the Holy Spirit in entire sanctification, Clarke, the crisis moment of entire sanctification, and Watson, the gradual aspect.[33] Using the Wesleyan motifs of circumcision of the heart and perfect love, Fletcher correlates entire sanctification to pentecostal baptism with the Holy Spirit.[34] His treatment of Christian perfection carries an explicit pneumatological emphasis uncharacteristic of Wesley's thought.[35] The correspondence of entire sanctification with pentecostal baptism gave the experience prominence over other elements of the *ordo salutis*. Clarke stresses instantaneity for both pardon and cleansing.[36] He suggests that a delay in being entirely sanctified must be due to the believer's spiritual laxity and lack of faith. Watson shows preference for process. He understands entire sanctification as a reasonable outcome of consistent growth in grace. However, for Watson, the process does not necessarily culminate in an instantaneous work.[37] These shifts towards one pole or the other in the salvific continuum were precursors for developments in the American terrain, in which they were further accentuated by different factions.

The American Holiness Movement arose within American Methodism and, over the course of the nineteenth century, spread to other theological traditions. At its inception in the 1760s, American Methodism emphasized the doctrine of Christian perfection as taught

32. William Burton Pope was a major theological figure in English Methodism whose teaching remained close to Wesley's. (Greathouse and Bassett, *Historical Development*, 255).

33. Peters, *Christian Perfection*, 107–8.

34. Fletcher, Works, 2: 141–42.

35. Wood, "Pentecostal Sanctification," 255. Wood (see also *Meaning of Pentecost*) and Dieter ("Nineteenth-Century Holiness Theology," 67) argue that Fletcher did not introduce a new teaching, but was merely explicit about an implicit connection in Wesley. Knight ("John Fletcher's Influence"), on the other hand, argues, "Wesley felt that Fletcher's sharp distinction between justification and initial sanctification, on the one hand, and the baptism of the Holy Spirit, on the other, implies that one does not receive the Holy Spirit in justification and initial sanctification. . . . Wesley did not distinguish between 'receiving the Holy Spirit' and 'being baptized with the Holy Spirit' as some in the holiness movement have done. Nor did he connect Christian perfection or entire sanctification with Pentecost. Fletcher apparently was the first to make this identification" (ibid., 27). In similar vein, Neff ("Wesley and Fletcher") sees a pneumatological emphasis in Fletcher's thought in contrast to a christological emphasis in Wesley's.

36. Mitchell, *Wesley Century*, 345.

37. Taylor, *Leading Wesleyan Thinkers*, 28–31.

by Wesley, with Fletcher's teaching of Spirit baptism as a subordinate concept.[38] According to some scholars, over the next several decades, interest in Christian perfection declined as the denomination focused on church expansion.[39] Furthermore, mainline Methodism tended to accentuate the gradual aspect of Christian perfection over the crisis experience of entire sanctification.[40] In response to this situation, in the 1830s and early 1840s, some prominent Methodists began to promote holiness teaching with emphasis on the crisis of entire sanctification. The Holiness Movement was born as the teaching gained numerical support and became increasingly widespread.[41]

The revivalist milieu into which holiness teaching was introduced was characterized by a sense of urgency, individualism and optimism in human endeavor. This shaped the way in which holiness was propagated.[42] Revivalism created an atmosphere of urgency in seeking religious experience. As Greathouse observes, "nineteenth-century revivalism sharpened the emphasis on 'the second blessing' and stressed the urgency and possibility of being sanctified *now*."[43] Preaching that urged immediate entire sanctification led to the need for a simple method to obtain the experience.

38. Greathouse and Bassett, *Historical Development*, 268; Dieter, "Nineteenth-Century Holiness Theology," 268–69.

39. Peters, *Christian Perfection*, 97–99; Dieter, *Holiness Revival*, 22. More recent scholarship indicates that interest in entire sanctification had continued, and that the 1830s phenomenon signified increased emphasis on what had already been a distinctive element of Methodist teaching (Coppedge, "Entire Sanctification," 34).

40. For example, in 1847 the first systematic theology of American Methodism was published by Thomas N. Ralston who writes, "It matters but little whether this eminent state of holiness be gained by a bold, energetic, and determined exercise of faith and prayer, or by a more gradual process—whether it be instantaneous or gradual, or both the one and the other." (Taylor, *Leading Wesleyan Thinkers*, 89.)

41. Powell, "Theological Significance," 127; George, "Selfhood and the Search for an Identity," 2–3. Powell identifies four phases in the nineteenth-century Holiness Movement. The promotion of holiness teaching within Methodism during the third and fourth decades of the nineteenth century marked the first phase. The formation of the National Camp Meeting Association for the Promotion of Holiness in 1867 marked the second phase. Mounting tensions between the Holiness Association and mainline Methodism during the 1870s marked the third phase. The fourth phase, in the late nineteenth century, was characterized by increasing independence of the Association from mainline Methodism. The outcome of these developments was the formation of Holiness denominations that inherited the nineteenth-century model of holiness ("Theological Significance," 127–33).

42. Bassett, "Theological Identity," 74.

43. Greathouse and Bassett, *Historical Development*, 296.

This contributed to the appeal of Palmer's "shorter way" teaching, which will be discussed in the following section. Individualism and optimism introduced an element of human volition into the concept of faith. Daniel Berg remarks that the freedom of the will "was an uncritiqued presupposition" of revivalism.[44] In the revivalist milieu, personal religious experience through human agency became a matter of primary importance.

These elements of the cultural context entered the stream of holiness teaching through revivalism. The combination of these developments resulted in a paradigm shift in holiness theology.[45]

Entire Sanctification in the Nineteenth-Century Holiness Movement

Phoebe Palmer emerged as a significant advocate of entire sanctification during this period. Through her books, periodical, weekly meetings, and preaching, Palmer reached hundreds of thousands with the message of holiness.[46] She held to the basic teaching of Wesley, but she nuanced the teaching with the elements of human decisiveness and urgency. White summarizes:

> Phoebe Palmer simplified and popularized John Wesley's doctrine of entire sanctification, modifying it in six different ways. First, she followed John Fletcher in his identification of entire sanctification with the baptism of the Holy Spirit. Second, she developed Adam Clarke's suggestion and linked holiness with power. Third, like Clarke, she stressed the instantaneous elements of sanctification to the exclusion of the gradual. Fourth, again following Clarke, she taught that entire sanctification is not the goal of the Christian life, but rather its beginning. Fifth, through her "altar theology" she reduced the attainment of sanctification to a straightforward three-stage process of entire consecration, faith, and testimony. Sixth, she held that one needed no evidence other than the Biblical text to be assured of entire sanctification.[47]

---

44. Berg, "Theological Context," 49–50.

45. Greathouse and Bassett, *Historical Development*, 296.

46. White "Phoebe Palmer," 198.

47. Ibid., 198.

This teaching gained a strong following through Palmer's clear and widespread propagation.[48] Palmer's teaching provides insight into the alterations to Wesley's teaching during the nineteenth century. These changes produced a teaching that abstracted entire sanctification from its theological grounding, introduced empowerment as the goal of the experience and human volition into the concept of faith. Furthermore, the content of the teaching focused on a method that believers could follow in order to be entirely sanctified. The result was a self-referential theology.

Dissociation from the Ordo Salutis

The explication of entire sanctification in this period shows theological, biblical and experiential abstraction. Theologically, the work of the Holy Spirit came to be associated with the pentecostal baptism of the Holy Spirit. The work of the Holy Spirit was primarily understood as entire sanctification. In contrast, as Greathouse observes, Wesley located entire sanctification within an *ordo salutis* of a threefold work of the Holy Spirit (prevenient grace, regeneration, and sanctification).[49] The Pentecost-entire sanctification correspondence diminished the importance the work of the Spirit in justification and gradual sanctification.

In addition, the primary exegetical foundation for entire sanctification in the Pentecost paradigm was the Acts of the Apostles rather than the whole scope of Scripture.[50] Wesley, on the other hand, made comprehensive use of Old and New Testaments to support the doctrine of Christian perfection. Furthermore, the popular understanding of entire sanctification was often read back into Scripture.[51] As a result of this hermeneutic, entire sanctification came to be understood in terms of a particular form of religious experience.

Experientially, the view of entire sanctification as the gateway to holiness minimized the import of justification and gradual sanctification in the life of the believer. As entire sanctification became the focal point of the Christian life, the wider soteriological framework characteristic of Wesley's teaching was obscured. According to Dieter, Palmer's teaching "tended to shift the point of balance away from that which Wesley had

48. Dayton, "Asa Mahan," 63.

49. Greathouse and Bassett, *Historical Development*, 307.

50. Dayton, "Asa Mahan," 65.

51. Hynson, "Wesleyan Quadrilateral," 21–22.

maintained and moved it closer to the crisis polarity and away from the gradualism and growth which formed the other pole of his dialectic."[52] By minimizing gradual sanctification, Palmer's teaching revised "the continuum of salvation within which Wesley had envisioned the experience."[53] Thus, as Dayton observes, holiness teaching accentuated the event of entire sanctification rather than the life of holiness.[54]

The dissociation of the entire sanctification experience from the *ordo salutis* and the whole salvific work of the Spirit accentuated the crisis character of the teaching. The experience was advanced as the means of becoming holy. Furthermore, divine freedom and grace were lost from view because the teaching developed a single form for divine action. Without the horizon of divine freedom and grace, the teaching collapsed into the sphere of a single experience.

The Goal of Empowerment

In tandem with its association with pentecostal baptism, entire sanctification came to be understood as a source of empowerment. The baptism of the Holy Spirit was understood as an experience of empowerment for holy living and effective witness.[55] Believers were encouraged to seek their personal Pentecost *for* the benefits of the experience. This introduced the idea of the Holy Spirit as a source of efficacy rather than as the personal presence of God. Moreover, the teaching urged believers to seek their personal pentecostal baptism, resulting in a limited view of the ecclesial significance of the Pentecost event.[56] Overall, entire sanctification and the work of the Spirit took on a personalistic and utilitarian aspect that showed little resemblance to Wesley's teaching of wholehearted love.

The Shorter Way

Based on her own experience,[57] Palmer taught that, through faith and consecration, the believer could experience entire sanctification without an

52. Dieter, "Nineteenth-Century Holiness Theology," 63.

53. Ibid., 63.

54. Dayton, "Asa Mahan," 66.

55. Greathouse and Bassett, *Historical Development*, 309.

56. Hynson, "The Wesleyan Quadrilateral," 19.

57. Palmer, *Way of Holiness*, 26–35.

extended period of gradual sanctification. She reasoned that faith meant taking God at His word, as recorded in the Bible. Dieter explains that for Palmer, since Scripture was the voice of God, if one acted on the basis of divine promise, one could expect fulfillment of the promise. Complete consecration meant placing one's self entirely on the altar, Christ being the Christian's altar.[58] Since the altar sanctifies the gift, Palmer reasoned that the fully consecrated believer could claim the blessing of entire sanctification.[59] As such, there was no reason to delay seeking the experience. For Palmer, since sanctification is God's will for us, and His time is always "now", one could expect to be entirely sanctified upon full consecration.[60] She also asserted that failure to seek the experience constituted unbelief and disobedience.[61] Furthermore, it was the duty of the entirely sanctified to publicly witness to the experience.[62]

Revivalist urgency and the pragmatic bent of popular American culture at the time provided fertile ground for Palmer's teaching. The outcome was that entire sanctification was widely understood as an experience that was readily available through an accessible method. Palmer herself was convinced that faith and consecration were only possible by grace.[63] Nonetheless, the practical result of her method-oriented teaching was that entire sanctification was possible upon the application of her proposed method, which suggested that the experience was under human control. Thus, although Palmer presupposed grace, the teaching she delivered did not sufficiently accentuate entire sanctification as a work of grace. In sum, entire sanctification depended on the believer's decisiveness.

Faith and Human Agency

The shorter way teaching adopted and reinforced the prevalent view of faith in the revivalist milieu. The tendency to a volitional view of faith, evident in the revivalist context, was fertile ground for Palmer's correlation

58. Dieter, "Nineteenth-Century Holiness Theology," 63 (hence the term "altar theology").

59. Ibid., 63; Greathouse and Bassett, *Historical Development*, 299.

60. Thus, Palmer's method was called "shorter way." Ibid., 299.

61. Dieter, "Nineteenth-Century Holiness Theology," 63.

62. Ibid.

63. Leclerc, "Phoebe Palmer," 96; Dieter, "Nineteenth-Century Holiness Theology," 62; Greathouse and Bassett, *Historical Development*, 300; Lowery, "Fork in the Wesleyan Road," 190; Powell, "Theological Significance," 127.

of faith with assent to scripture.[64] Faith was simply a decision to take God at His word. Lowery remarks that on Palmer's view, failure to experience holiness was due to the believer's lack of decisiveness.[65] Thus, the shorter way equated faith with intellectual assent to Scripture.

This stands in stark contrast to Wesley's view of faith as a gift. As shown earlier in this chapter, Wesley's concept of faith is fundamental to the doctrine of Christian perfection. The transformation of the concept of faith which arose under Palmer's influence meant that a radically different epistemology underlay the doctrine of holiness.[66] The transformed concept of faith also had wider implications for the Wesleyan concept of inherited sin, and the priority of divine grace in Wesleyan soteriology. Palmer's view of faith accentuated the individual's ability to believe without explicitly affirming moral capacity as a function of grace. The practical outcome was a view of entire sanctification as act of will rather than gift of grace.[67]

Signs of Subjectivism

These nineteenth-century modifications shaped holiness teaching into a anthropocentric framework. The correlation of entire sanctification with pentecostal baptism with the Holy Spirit introduced a pneumatology that focused on entire sanctification rather than the whole work of salvation. Furthermore, the teaching focused on urging believers to seek the baptism with the Holy Spirit as a means of personal empowerment. This introduced a utilitarian and individualistic view of the work of grace. The promotion of entire sanctification as instantaneously available by faith and consecration, and these understood as decisive human actions, resulted in a holiness doctrine that stressed human agency over divine grace. Palmer's theology advanced a formulaic approach to obtaining entire sanctification. The result was a person-oriented teaching that undermined entire sanctification as a work of divine grace.

---

64. Palmer, *Way of Holiness*, 36–37.
65. Lowery, "Fork in the Wesleyan Road," 194.
66. Dieter, "Nineteenth-Century Holiness Theology," 64.
67. Bassett, "Theological Identity," 75; Berg, "Theological Context," 48.

Current Holiness Theology

The principal theological endeavor in the twentieth century was to articulate a biblically sound teaching in harmony with Wesleyan and Holiness Movement roots. The proposals that ensued addressed the crisis-process relation as well as the correspondence of entire sanctification with pentecostal baptism. While there was greater clarity regarding these issues, there are now two main approaches to holiness theology, both developed in terms of personal religious experience.

Twentieth-Century Developments

In subsequent decades of the nineteenth century, theological polarization and organizational tension led to increasing dichotomy between the Holiness Movement and mainline Methodism.[68] The main point of controversy was that the Holiness associations propagated entire sanctification as their central and single issue.[69] Late nineteenth and early twentieth centuries saw the formation of holiness denominations independent from Methodism.[70]

During the twentieth century, holiness theologies modified nineteenth-century views of faith, the relation of entire sanctification to the *ordo salutis* and the baptism with the Holy Spirit. As a result, by the end of the century, holiness theology reflected Wesley's construal more than had been evident in the nineteenth century.

In the early twentieth century, the concept of faith was initially characterized by a strong affirmation of moral freedom that diminished the need for enabling grace.[71] Later theologies of the twentieth century moved away from this perspective and sought to retrieve the concept of faith as a divine gift. While free agency was still implicit in the revised concept of faith, it was understood as gracious ability rather than natural ability.[72]

Mid-century, reawakened interest in Wesley brought to light departures from his teaching that had been inherited from the nineteenth

---

68. Dieter, "Nineteenth-Century Holiness Theology," 66; Powell, "Theological Significance," 130–31. This conflict began in the 1830s and continued until the schisms of the late nineteenth and early twentieth centuries (Schneider, "Conflict of Associations," 270).

69. Dieter, "Nineteenth-Century Holiness Theology," 65.

70. Smith, *Called Unto Holiness*, 2: 27.

71. Bassett, "Theology of the Early Holiness Movement," 71.

72. Wiley, *Christian Theology*, 2: 475.

century.[73] This resulted in theological projects to retrieve Wesley's vision of Christian perfection. Thus, the *ordo salutis* obtained renewed significance. Theologies emerged that linked entire sanctification with justification and gradual sanctification. Wiley, for example, clarifies the distinctions and connections between justification and entire sanctification. Regeneration "is the bestowal of divine life, and as an operation of the Spirit, is complete in itself."[74] It is the impartation of the life of love.[75] Entire sanctification is heart purification and infilling with perfect love.[76] While regeneration marks the beginning of new life in Christ through the Holy Spirit, entire sanctification marks the beginning of a life of perfect love through cleansing from inbred sin and the fullness of the Holy Spirit.

The association of entire sanctification with Pentecost was called into question as the century progressed.[77] The principal argument against the correlation is New Testament evidence that believers receive the Holy Spirit in regeneration. By the end of the century, scholars seemed to have reached consensus that in the new birth the believer receives the Holy Spirit and in entire sanctification the believer is filled with the Spirit.

The twentieth century saw a reintegration of entire sanctification into its soteriological framework of origin. Entire sanctification continued to be taught as a critical crisis experience in the life of holiness, necessary for cleansing from inbred sin. However, this experience was reconnected to justification and gradual sanctification. The Pentecost paradigm was nuanced to achieve stronger harmony with Scripture. Entire sanctification was explicated in terms that acknowledged the prevenient, justifying and sanctifying works of the Holy Spirit. Nonetheless, as pointed out in chapter 1, holiness theology continues to manifest a strand of subjectivism.

73. Reasoner, "The American Holiness Movement's Paradigm Shift," 140.

74. Wiley, *Christian Theology*, 2: 475.

75. Ibid., 476.

76. Ibid.

77. The debate can be traced in both 1979 issues of the Wesleyan Theological Journal: Lyon, "Spirit-Baptism in the New Testament"; Deasley "Entire Sanctification and Baptism"; Turner "Baptism of the Holy Spirit"; Wynkoop, "Theological Roots"; Agnew, "Baptized with the Spirit"; Arnett, "The Role of the Holy Spirit"; Grider, "Spirit Baptism"; Wood, "Exegetical-Theological Reflections."

The Self-Referential Strand in Current Holiness Theology

The primary concerns addressed in the twentieth century concern the believer's personal experience of entire sanctification. While this is a valid practical consideration, exclusive attention to this dimension of holiness theology reduces the sphere of reflection to religious experience and ethics. This section discusses the fundamental problem of holiness theology as outlined in the previous chapter. In treatments of entire sanctification, continued crisis-process tension, emphasis on the proximate rather than transcendent goal of the experience, prominence of the believer's role, and limited consideration of the ecclesial significance of the doctrine are evidences of the self-referential paradigm.

As discussed earlier, explications of entire sanctification accentuate either crisis or process. From the crisis point of view, the experience is understood as an instantaneous work of the Holy Spirit that cleanses the believer from inherited sin. From the process perspective, perfection connotes maturity, so that the believer continues to grow in grace throughout life without the necessity of a second work of grace. One reason for this ambiguity is the subjectivist orientation of current holiness theology. In the nineteenth century, crisis was accentuated on the grounds of the Pentecost paradigm, the shorter way teaching and the urgency of revivalism. In current theology, crisis has come to be understood as an anomaly because it is interpreted as the form of religious experience that arose in the nineteenth century.[78] Thus, the critique of crisis is based upon an understanding of the concept as an element of the form rather the theological content of holiness theology. This approach shows that theological reflection continues to move within the subjective context.

Some explications of entire sanctification consider the proximate rather than the transcendent goal of the experience. The proximate goal is moral transformation. As such, person-centered explications present the experience as the way to be made holy. Such explications include extended treatments of how to obtain the experience. Emphasis on the believer's role without explicit affirmation of the graced-ness of the experience produces a self-referential theology. On this view, the experiencing subject is the primary reference, which overshadows the ultimate goal and possibility of human holiness. Moreover, subjectivism can lead to spiritual self-involvement and unhealthy preoccupation with personal

---

78. Dunning, "Toward a New Paradigm," 154.

spirituality. This limits the vision of holiness to the individual, and cuts off the orientation to the other, which is the very hallmark of holiness.

The implications of holiness doctrine tend to be restricted to the area of Christian ethics.[79] Limiting the relevance of the teaching to ethics reinforces its individualistic orientation. Recent reformulations of holiness theology emphasize this ethical reading. Augello reformulates entire sanctification by combining Wesley's concept of "holy affections" with the Roman Catholic concept of virtue habituation, as understood in the Aristotelian-Thomistic tradition.[80] Colón-Emeric compares the concept of Christian perfection in Wesley and Aquinas.[81] Colón-Emeric's project stresses the significance of holiness to the church catholic. He shows the complementarity between the speculative treatment of holiness by Aquinas, and the practical treatment by Wesley. These treatments of Wesley's Christian Perfection, while fruitful for spiritual formation, reinforce the perception of holiness theology as limited to the moral sphere.

It may be argued that entire sanctification *is* a human experience and should be considered as such. Holiness teaching should speak to the practical application in the life of the believer. Without this experiential axis, there is danger of obscuring the transformative power of grace and the importance of experiential knowledge of God. Yet, entire sanctification is more than a human experience. It points to the astounding reality of divine holiness and condescension, and the real possibility of participation in God. Thus, theological reflection must reach beyond the human experience to the wider horizon of divine holiness and the divine salvific mission. As chapter 3 will show, such an approach offers more potential for a theologically robust articulation that would be sustainable as the distinctive teaching of the Wesleyan-Holiness tradition.

Conclusion

This chapter set out to trace the shifts in holiness theology from Wesley's teaching to the present. While Wesley grounded entire sanctification in an *ordo salutis* characterized by a crisis-process balance, the nineteenth-century Holiness Movement adopted Wesley's teaching with a marked preference for the crisis pole. The crisis orientation in the context of revivalism

79. Wiley, *Christian Theology*, 3: 7–100.
80. Augello, "Wesleyan-Holiness Movement's Doctrine."
81. Colón-Emeric, "Perfection in Dialogue."

and individualism led to a subjective understanding of the doctrine. The focus of holiness teaching was limited to the believer's experience of entire sanctification. Furthermore, the concept of faith underwriting the Holiness Movement project assimilated the volitional focus of popular American culture. Faith was understood more as an act of will and less as a gift of grace. Current holiness teaching locates entire sanctification in the Wesleyan *ordo salutis*, and underscores the need for gradual sanctification. Nonetheless, the standard theological approach begins with the experiencing subject and develops along the lines of personal spirituality. One way of breaking free of subjectivism is to approach the doctrine from the standpoint of its ultimate rather than proximate goal. This suggests a consideration of holiness theology in terms of communion with God. Such an approach would not preclude consideration of the personal significance of entire sanctification. Instead, it would locate the subjective aspect of holiness theology within the transcendent goal of the divine salvific mission. The next chapter introduces a paradigm that seeks to extend theological reflection to the transcendent goal of entire sanctification.

3

The Communion Paradigm

Introduction

As discussed in the previous chapter, Wesley's experiential theology shifted into a self-referential paradigm within the nineteenth-century Holiness Movement. Twentieth-century theology sought to harmonize two conceptions of entire sanctification. Although fruitful in may respects, this project has not resulted in a single, commonly held view of entire sanctification. The approach was to reconcile discrete elements of the teaching but this has not produced a single articulation of holiness theology that honors both strands of the tradition. I have argued that subjectivism, which continues to characterize holiness theology, is the fundamental reason for the present ambiguity. The problem thus construed suggests the need to approach holiness theology from a standpoint common to both strands of the tradition and to break away from the self-referential paradigm.

The aim of this chapter is to demonstrate that consideration of holiness theology from the perspective of communion with God dissolves the self-referential paradigm without negating the contributions of the nineteenth century. Communion with God is an appropriate starting point because it is the core of Wesleyan soteriology. The communion perspective allows adequate recognition of the nuances given to Wesley's thought in later Methodism and in the Holiness Movement. It frees holiness theology from subjectivism while safeguarding its experiential character. It extends the sphere of reflection beyond personal religious experience and suggests a wider definition of holiness theology.

By considering both received articulations of entire sanctification, the first section of this chapter demonstrates that the goal of entire sanctification is fullness of communion with God. By drawing out the implications of this transcendent goal, the second section sketches a paradigm for holiness theology. Finally, by comparison with an alternative proposal, the third section shows the adequacy of the communion paradigm.

Fullness of Communion and Entire Sanctification

Communion refers to participation in God, or personal knowledge of God. Accordingly, as Wood remarks, "We know God in relation, in creative and transformative activity. We also know ourselves in God. Personal knowledge is characterized by this reciprocity."[1] The idea of participation in relation to sanctification is an enduring theme in Scripture.[2] The motif "in Christ" in the thought of St. Paul represents a union of love, in which Paul's "I want to know Christ" means "I want to draw near in fellowship."[3] Likewise, in the Johannine writings, the knowledge of God is fellowship with God. "The believer who knows God has received the gift of God which is love; there is an inner binding of the believer who knows God and God Who is known. By our knowledge of God we are actually in the heart of God."[4] The knowledge of communion is also associated with sanctification in the thought of Clement of Alexandria, Augustine, Aquinas, and others.[5] In sum, *amor ipse notitia est* is attested by both Scripture and Christian tradition.[6] Thus, the communion approach connects holiness theology with a significant biblical and theological theme that transcends the Wesleyan-Holiness tradition.

Consideration of communion with God in the thought of John Wesley and Phineas Bresee reveals the deep harmony of the two streams of the Wesleyan-Holiness tradition. Wesley is the architect of the doctrine of Christian perfection with which this book is concerned. Wesley's

1. Wood, "The Liturgy," 96.

2. Flew shows the association between the knowledge of communion and perfection in Scripture and tradition: Paul, John, Clement of Alexandria, Augustine, Aquinas and others.

3. Flew, *The Idea of Perfection*, 48.

4. Ibid., 102.

5. Ibid., 146; 200; 240–41.

6. "Love is itself knowledge" (Gregory the Great, *Homilia in Evangelium* 27; PL 76:1207a).

heart religion is essentially transformative fellowship with God culminating in Christian perfection through entire sanctification. The sermons of Phineas Bresee reflect the holiness theology of the early twentieth century. In his thought, all prior knowledge of God is for the sake of intimate union with Christ through entire sanctification. Common to both Wesley and Bresee is that communion with God reaches fullness through the experience of entire sanctification.

In sum, communion with God is an appropriate perspective from which to develop holiness theology. It is the core of the Wesleyan soteriological vision, transcending particular nuances adopted by Wesley's theological descendants. In view of the task at hand, retrieval of the communion theme offers the potential of a holiness theology that brings the experiential focus to the forefront of reflection and dissolves the self-referential paradigm.

John Wesley

The previous chapter explicated Wesley's *ordo salutis* as the soteriological framework in which entire sanctification arises. The following discussion demonstrates that this framework is dynamic and transformative, because it is essentially participation in God by faith. Fellowship with God is a spiritual sphere of increasing knowledge of God by faith. The *ordo salutis* is marked by two moments—conversion and entire sanctification—that change the character of the divine-human relation. Conversion marks the beginning of fellowship with God through reconciliation; entire sanctification marks the beginning of fullness of communion or Christian perfection.

The essence of heart religion is fellowship with God. It is the transcendent purpose of life and the source of happiness.[7] Albert Outler describes "Circumcision of the Heart" as the sermon in which Wesley "spells out the theme of the Christian's participation in God as the essence of Christian existence."[8] In this sermon, Wesley asserts that fellowship with the Father and the Son in the Holy Spirit is the transcendent goal of human existence, the *summum bonum*.[9] The fundamental characteristic of a genuine Christian is inexpressible happiness arising from the conviction that the "all-powerful, all-wise, all-gracious Being, this Governor of

---

7. "What is Man," Psalm 8:4, *Works* VII: 230.

8. Outler and Heitzenrater, *An Anthology* , 23.

9. "Circumcision of the Heart," *Works* V: 207–8.

all, loves me. This Lover of my soul is always with me, is never absent, no, not for a moment. And I love Him."[10] Wood remarks, "For Wesley, man's greatest good is thus to be realized in the knowledge of God. Since knowledge is total involvement with reality, this means that to know God is to love God."[11] Thus, participation in God is heart religion.

Fellowship begins in conversion through the gift of faith, and thrives by increasing faith.[12] Wesley describes conversion as the moment when the Father reveals the Son in the heart of the believer. It is the first knowledge of Jesus Christ. At this moment, "real, solid, substantial" happiness begins. The source of this happiness is the knowledge of the love of God. As explained in chapter 2, Wesley describes faith as the awakening of spiritual senses and the knowledge that comes through these awakened senses. This knowledge is inward certitude of the love of God. Saving faith is personal knowledge of God's love, manifested in Jesus Christ, and actualized in the believer's heart by the Holy Spirit.[13] Realization of the love of God brings the capacity to love Him since "it is in consequence of our knowing God loves us, that we love him, and love our neighbour as ourselves."[14] As Johnson observes, for Wesley, faith in God leads to knowledge of God and both faith and knowledge become the ground for the self's genuine love for God.[15] Thus, the moment of conversion is

10 "Letter to Conyers Middleton," *Works* X: 71.

11. Wood, "Wesley's Epistemology," 57.

12. The term conversion refers to the crisis moment of justification by faith and regeneration. In the "New Birth," Wesley shows the relation between justification and regeneration, and these two, to sanctification. Justification refers to the "work God does for us, in forgiving our sins" (*Works* VI: 65). Regeneration, also referred to as the new birth, is the "work God does *in* us, in renewing our fallen nature" (ibid., 65). He clarifies that these two works occur in the same experience, which, in this discussion, is referred to as conversion. Nonetheless, in terms of priority, "justification precedes the new birth. We first conceive his wrath to be turned away, and then his Spirit to work in our hearts" (ibid., 65–66). Furthermore, "the new birth is not the same with sanctification" (ibid., 74). Instead, the new birth is "the gate" to sanctification. Wesley states, "When we are born again, then our sanctification, our inward and outward holiness, begins" (ibid., 74). He uses the analogy of natural birth and subsequent growth to describe the distinction between the new birth and sanctification. The former is a precise moment, while the latter is a process. He concludes, "The same relation, therefore, which there is between our natural birth and our growth, there is also between our new birth and our sanctification" (ibid., 75).

13. "Circumcision of the Heart," *Works* V: 205.

14. "The Unity of the Divine Being," *Works* VII: 269.

15. Johnson, "Christian Perfection as Love for God," 51–52.

nothing short of a personal revelation of the love of God, which launches the believer into a spiritual sphere of existence characterized by conviction of the love, acceptance and forgiveness of God through Christ.

Communion with God is transformative because realization of the love of God brings happiness and a sense of belonging.[16] This enables the believer to love others.[17] Johnson shows that, for Wesley, fellowship with God is an ever-flowing wellspring, which finds deepening expression in love for God and one's neighbor.[18] Thus, personal knowledge of God imparts the capacity to engage in fruitful relationships. This transformation begins in conversion and continues as fellowship with God deepens and the believer grows up in the knowledge of God. Heart religion, or true religion, refers to the transformative impact of fellowship with God.[19] True religion is union with Christ, fellowship with the triune God, eternal life in the present. It is the "knowledge and love of God, manifested in the Son of his love, through the eternal Spirit."[20] True religion, or heart religion, is the life of faith: "The life of faith, the knowledge of God, is such love for God that God is the desire of the eyes, the joy of the heart, one's portion in time and in eternity."[21] The "heart" of heart religion is this joyful fellowship with God. Its transformative impact is evidenced by a disposition of "lowliness, meekness, and resignation."[22] This alone is "life which is hid with Christ in God." He alone who experiences this "dwells in God and God in him."[23]

Deepening fellowship comes through a divine-human dialogue in which God gives Himself to be known, and the believer responds to God by faith. The grace of divine self-giving, objectively expressed in Christ, is actualized in the believer's life through the Holy Spirit. Wesley describes the work of the Spirit as "a continual action of God upon the soul, and a reaction of the soul upon God; an unceasing presence of God, the loving, pardoning God, manifested to the heart, and perceived by faith."[24] In fellowship with God, by use of the spiritual senses, the believer increases

16. "Scriptural Christianity," *Works* V: 39.

17. "Spiritual Worship," *Works* VI: 430.

18. Johnson, "Christian Perfection as Love for God," 52.

19. "Sermon on the Mount: Discourse II," *Works* V: 268.

20. "Spiritual Worship," *Works* VI: 432.

21. "Scriptural Christianity," *Works* V: 40.

22. "Walking by Sight, and Walking by Faith," *Works* VII: 263.

23. Ibid.

24. "Born of God," *Works* V: 232.

daily in the knowledge of God through "a kind of spiritual respiration" that sustains the life of God in the soul.[25]

This grace-enabled divine-human dialogue requires ongoing receptivity to the Holy Spirit. "God does not continue to act upon the soul, unless the soul re-acts upon God."[26] Prior to conversion, God "calls us to himself, and shines upon our hearts."[27] In the conversion experience, "he first loves us and manifests himself unto us."[28] However, genuine fellowship requires a human response to the Holy Spirit, which is itself enabled by the Holy Spirit. Wesley asserts that the Holy Spirit "will not continue to breathe into our soul, unless our soul breathes toward him again; unless our love, and prayer, and thanksgiving return to him, a sacrifice wherewith he is well pleased."[29] Grace-enabled human response allows the believer to engage in genuine fellowship with God.

Divine-human indwelling reaches fullness, wherein the believer's participation in God becomes wholehearted. Relationally understood, fullness refers to a qualitative difference in communion with God. Completeness in Christ means being filled with God.[30] It is dwelling "in Christ and Christ in us," being one with Christ and Christ with us.[31] It is God's unrivalled reign in the believer's heart. Fullness in the divine-human fellowship is, from the believer's standpoint, exclusive loyalty and devotion to one Lord. Fullness of communion corresponds to Wesley's description of Christian perfection: wholehearted love for God and one's neighbor—love for God for His own sake, and love for one's neighbor for God's sake. To love God is to desire Him, desire to please Him, and to find our happiness in Him.[32] It is the singular reign of pure love in the heart and life.[33] The believer who is made perfect in love is freed from self-will and desires nothing but "the holy and perfect will of God."[34] Thus, fullness of communion is a life of love and obedience to God, which finds expression in love for one's neighbor. This quality in divine-human fellowship

25. "The New Birth," *Works* VI: 70.

26. "Born of God," *Works* V: 233.

27. Ibid.

28. Ibid.

29. "The Privilege of those that are Born of God," *Works* V: 233.

30. "Spiritual Worship," *Works* VI: 430–31.

31. Ibid.

32. "On Love," *Works* VII: 495.

33. "Plain Account," *Works* XI: 401.

34. Ibid., 379.

requires entire sanctification since inherited sin stands in contradiction to communion with God.

Inherited sin is a principle of unbelief that remains in the believer subsequent to regeneration.[35] Wesley argues convincingly that all the Christian creeds attest to the continued presence of the sin principle in the life of the regenerate. Outler notes that for Wesley, "at justification, the believer is delivered from the dominion of outward sin, but although the power of inward sin is broken, it is by no means destroyed."[36] Thus, "a depth of sin" remains in the believer.[37] Inherited sin is, fundamentally, a principle of unbelief. Sinfulness is due to a shift of allegiance from God to the devil.[38] "The very essence of unbelief lies in departing from God, as the *living God*—the fountain of all our life, holiness, happiness."[39] Collins remarks that for Wesley, "the nature of human sin, its irreducible essence, is . . . unbelief, the perversion of a relationship between God and humanity. A lack of faith in God . . . is the true foundation for the subsequent evils of pride and self-will."[40] Unbelief is an obstacle to wholehearted love for God, and for this reason, the cleansing experience of entire sanctification is necessary for fullness of communion.

The obstacle of inherited sin becomes increasingly apparent as the believer progresses in the life of faith. Believers experience deep conviction of the carnal mind, which is enmity against God.[41] The Holy Spirit reveals the tendency to self-will, pride and uncharitableness in one's thoughts, words, and actions.[42] In all these ways, inbred sin constitutes a principle that is contrary to love. The practical effect is that a conflict arises between the believer's desire to love God wholeheartedly and the antithetical principle that strives against this desire.[43]

Freedom from sin comes through repentance and faith in justification and entire sanctification. For Wesley, faith and repentance are not only necessary for justification. He insists, "It is generally supposed that repentance and faith are only the gate of religion; that they are necessary

35 "Sin in Believers," *Works* V: 144–56.

36. Outler and Heitzenrater, *An Anthology*, 405.

37. "Repentance of Believers," *Works* V: 169.

38. "Fall of Man," *Works* VI: 216–17.

39. Wesley, *Notes Upon the New Testament*, 570.

40. Collins, *Holy Love*, 58–59.

41 "Repentance of Believers," *Works* V: 169.

42. Ibid., 158–62.

43. Ibid., 163.

only at the beginning of our Christian course, when we are setting out in the way of the kingdom."[44] Instead, they are elements of the life of communion with God. "There is also a repentance and a faith which are requisite after we have 'believed the gospel'; yea, and in every subsequent stage of our Christian course, or we cannot 'run the race which is set before us.'"[45] Accordingly, repentance and faith draw unbelievers to justification and believers to entire sanctification.

Repentance includes conviction of inbred sin, guiltiness before God, and helplessness. Conviction is both recognition of, and loathing for, inbred sin. The guilt of the believer is the conviction of deserving divine condemnation, but not being so condemned entirely on account of the provision and intercession of Jesus Christ.[46] Helplessness is the persuasion of one's inability to be rid of sin, "which we experimentally know to *remain* in the heart, even of them that are regenerate," or to love God and our neighbor as we ought.[47] The combination of these convictions constrains the believer "to groan, for a full deliverance, to him that is mighty to save."[48]

Deliverance from inherited sin comes by faith, the particular conviction that God does cleanse away inherited sin through the merits of Christ and the action of the Holy Spirit. From the moment of justification, the believer continues in the justified state until there is faith for cleansing from indwelling sin. From the moment of cleansing, the believer continues in the state of fullness of communion with the full assurance of faith.[49] Cleansing is by faith in Christ as all in all; and since it is a work of grace by faith, it is the work of a moment.[50] Just as repentance and faith launched one into a life of fellowship with God in justification, repentance and faith bring the believer the Holy Spirit's cleansing from sin and the commencement of fullness of communion with God in entire sanctification.

Through repentance and faith, the Holy Spirit entirely sanctifies the believer. Wesley refers to entire sanctification as deliverance from all sin, both outward and inward, "from evil desires and evil tempers." This is circumcision of the heart, which frees the believer to love God

---

44. "Repentance of Believers," *Works* V: 156.

45. Ibid., 157.

46. Ibid., 163–64.

47. Ibid., 164.

48. Ibid., 169.

49. Ibid., 167.

50. Ibid., 170.

wholeheartedly.[51] Thus, entire sanctification is not only deliverance from inherited sin; it is the infusion of good dispositions and whole-hearted love for God.[52]

The foregoing discussion has shown that, for Wesley, the goal of salvation by faith is communion with God. Fullness of communion is wholehearted fellowship with God, which is made possible through entire sanctification. Cleansing from inherited sin frees the believer for fullness of communion. Thus, the goal of entire sanctification is to establish fullness of communion.

Phineas Bresee

The sermons of Phineas Bresee underscore the theme of intimate fellow-ship with God.[53] In the new birth, the believer comes to a preliminary knowledge of Jesus Christ by faith. In entire sanctification, the baptism with the Holy Spirit cleanses away inherited sin and brings the believer into intimate union with Christ. The purpose of entire sanctification is to draw the believer into fullness of communion.

The new birth is a preliminary knowledge of discovery of Jesus Christ as Savior. In "To Know Him," Bresee discusses St. Paul's conver-sion on the Damascus Road. The knowledge of discovery that comes to Paul is of Jesus Christ as the way to reconciliation to God and forgiveness of sins. Paul receives this knowledge through a personal manifestation of Jesus Christ. This knowledge is transformative. Bresee contends that Paul is "reconstructed" by his inward adjustment to the truth of Jesus Christ.[54] Yet, this discovery of Christ is only the beginning of fellowship with Him. While the knowledge of discovery is genuine knowledge, it is only a precursor of a deeper union with Christ.

---

51. "Plain Account," *Works* XI: 389 (As Deut 30:6 states, "The Lord your God will circumcise your hearts and the hearts of your descendants, so that you may love him with all your heart and with all your soul, and live").

52. "Discoveries of Faith," *Works* VII: 237.

53. See Ingersol, *Nazarene Roots*, 87–92 for Phineas Bresee's contribution to the Church of the Nazarene in the early twentieth century. His articulation of holiness theology instantiates the conviction, passion and vision of the holiness denominations that were formed in the late nineteenth and early twentieth centuries.

54. "To Know Him."

The knowledge of God comes by faith, which is "the soul's attitude of trustful obedience" to what God has revealed of Himself.[55] Faith is appropriation of the truths of revelation.[56] It is the gift of God. The believer gives heart-loyalty to Jesus Christ as the Holy Spirit reveals Christ to the heart. Christ strengthens the volition so that we can confess our sins. He enables the believer's heart surrender to Him. "He takes our wicked heart, which volition turns over to Him, and gives us a new heart—a heart to love Him, a heart which has the attitude of obedience to Him."[57] The revelation of Jesus Christ in Scripture is made manifest in the heart when Christ engages the believer in allegiance to Himself through the Holy Spirit.[58]

The knowledge of discovery marks the beginning of fellowship that flourishes as the Holy Spirit continues to reveal Christ in the heart of the believer.[59] "He who through the revelation of God by the Spirit has discovered the Christ, and taken his cross to follow Him, will find in and through the Word, by the Spirit, revelations and manifestations of his Lord to his own soul."[60] Like Wesley, Bresee speaks of the life of faith as a growing fellowship of deepening engagement with Christ. Growth in the knowledge of God brings deeper awareness of one's self. The Holy Spirit sheds light on the believer's lack of conformity to Christ, that is, "all things that hinder fullest fellowship with himself."[61] This is preparatory to the great moment in which God imparts to the believer the Gift of Himself.[62]

Divine self-giving is the central idea in Bresee's understanding of entire sanctification. The Spirit's baptism cleanses away inherited sin but this cleansing is *through* and *for* the divine indwelling. Baptism with the

55. "The Certainties of Faith."

56. Ibid.

57. "The Certainties of Faith." Chapter 2 showed that an element of human agency was introduced into the concept of faith in the nineteenth-century Holiness Movement. Bresee's definition of faith reflects this influence to some extent. He defines faith first, as a revelation of Christ to the believer's heart. This revelation empowers the will to subscribe to the truth of Jesus Christ by giving the heart to Him. Thus, although Bresee maintains a volitional element in his concept of faith, he also suggests that human agency is preceded by a prior divine movement.

58. Although Bresee reflects the pneumatological emphasis of the Holiness tradition, he also includes a christological focus by asserting that the work of the Spirit is to reveal Christ to the believer, and to draw the believer into union with Christ.

59. "To Know Him."

60. Ibid.

61. Ibid.

62. "The Outstretched Hands."

Holy Spirit is "the baptism with God. It is the burning up of the chaff, but it is also the revelation in us and the manifestation to us of Divine personality, filling our being."[63] Thus, the baptism with the Holy Spirit is an end in itself.[64] Cleansing from inherited sin is for the fullness of the in-dwelling Holy Spirit.[65] "The house is cleaned, purified, in order to receive the Guest. He makes it ready for His abode."[66] "Jesus sought for Himself fellowship, communion and unity with human souls. By this baptism, He is enthroned and revealed in man."[67] Thus, the transcendent goal of entire sanctification is fullness of communion with God through the fullness of the Holy Spirit's indwelling.

Fullness of communion is union with Christ. While the believer re-ceives the knowledge of discovery in the new birth, the knowledge of God in entire sanctification is participation in, or intimate union with Christ. Entire sanctification is the Holy Spirit's gift of Himself to the believer.[68] Therefore, the knowledge of God that comes in entire sanctification is a deeper participation in Christ. This is the knowledge of personality.[69] He clarifies, "Real knowledge of personality, at least the best knowledge of personality, comes from association, fellowship."[70] This fellowship is par-ticipation in the power of Christ's resurrection, which is experienced in the baptism with the Holy Spirit: "The power of the resurrection of Christ is the resident power of the Spirit. The Holy Ghost resident in man is God's dynamite in the soul."[71] It is also participation in the fellowship of the suf-fering of Christ. This means, for Bresee, participation in Christ's love for humanity. In other words, fellowship includes the idea of engagement in the standpoint of the other, for the sake of the other: "Not for the reward, not for the glory, but in very nature united with the infinite passion to lift men from the jaws of hell and save from the power of sin."[72] To know God is to be in union with Christ, to be caught up in His vision of reality, to

63. "Consuming Fire." See also "The Blessing" and "Transfiguring Gaze" for the theme of participation in God as the goal of the Spirit's baptism.

64. "Divine Power."

65. "The Transfiguring Gaze."

66. "The Great Question."

67. "The Blessing."

68. "The Outstretched Hands."

69. "One Thing."

70. "To Know Him."

71. Ibid.

72. Ibid.

dwell in a new sphere circumscribed by Christ Himself. This fellowship is the direct revelation of Christ in the heart, the fullness of divine indwelling.

Entire sanctification is the full actualization of God's plan of salvation, in the sense that it establishes the kind of relationship that God desires with His people. Salvation history is in view of this fellowship. "Patriarchal teaching; the law as a school-master for a distrustful people; the culmination of law and prophecy in John the Baptist; the incarnation of the Son of God, His death, resurrection, ascension, were all preparatory for the crowning, abiding glory of the Holy Ghost."[73] God's saving work in the hearts of individuals is also aimed at the fullness of the divine indwelling. The new birth in Christ is for the baptism with the Holy Spirit.[74] Entire sanctification is primarily the coming of the Comforter, a personal Pentecost. This experience is the center of God's salvific work, because it ushers in intimate union with Christ, which, subsequently, develops as the believer is "divinely enlarged and transformed."[75] Otherwise stated, the baptism with the Holy Spirit marks the beginning of singularity in the believer's devotion to Christ, which expands from this point onwards.

This exploration of Bresee's thought has shown that the new birth is a precursor of entire sanctification. The discoveries of the new birth come to fruition in entire sanctification. In entire sanctification, the Holy Spirit cleanses the believer from inherited sin and fills the believer's heart with His own presence. This experience is a revelation of God, which allows the believer to be in intimate communion with God. Thus, for Bresee, the goal of entire sanctification is intimate communion with God.

The Communion Paradigm

In the thought of both Wesley and Bresee, the goal of entire sanctification is fullness of divine-human communion. The central soteriological principle of both accounts is transformative fellowship with God. This commonality discloses the deep harmony of vision that transcends their divergent emphases. The singular vision of intimacy with God suggests an expansion in the conception of holiness theology to include its rootedness in the divine fellowship of holy love. It underscores the nature of entire sanctification as a gift of grace and as genuine reciprocity. It illuminates human holiness as

73. "The Outstretched Hands."
74. "The Blessing."
75. "Death and Life."

the outcome of fellowship with God, a process of becoming in which crisis occasions greater depths of love and knowledge. The experience of entire sanctification refers to the crisis occasion that ushers in fullness of communion. Accordingly, this section suggests the parameters of reflection for holiness theology that is oriented to fullness of communion.

The Triune Fellowship of Holy Love

The communion model explicitly connects holiness theology to the triune fellowship of holy love as its cause. This perspective enlarges the definition of holiness theology by extending reflection beyond the personal dimension. Essentially, thinking about entire sanctification as a threshold into complete openness to fellowship with God entails reflection upon the triune fellowship itself. In terms of theological construction, this introduces a trinitarian basis for holiness theology.

When considered in terms of divine-human fellowship, the logical starting point for holiness theology is the nature of God. The question necessarily arises, "What kind of God desires and enables fellowship with the creature?" According to Webster, "God's holiness is the majestic incomparability, difference and purity which he is in himself as Father, Son and Holy Spirit, and which is manifest and operative in the economy of his works in the love with which he elects, reconciles and perfects human partners for fellowship with himself."[76] Thus, "holiness and love are mutually conditioning and mutually illuminative terms, which can only be expounded in relation to each other, and which both serve as conceptual indicators of the being and ways of the triune God."[77] Similarly, Wiley describes the holiness of God as "the peculiar quality of that nature out of which love flows."[78] The outflow of God's holy nature reaches out to the creature for fellowship. Thus, holiness theology, which asserts the possibility of heart purity, can only be properly justified as it accounts for this possibility through reference to God's nature of holy love.

Explicating entire sanctification as the gateway to fullness of communion sheds light on divine holiness as the cause of the divine salvific mission and the guarantee of human holiness. Holiness circumscribes love with integrity. Thus, holy love is merciful and mighty, unassailable

---

76. Webster, "The Holiness and Love of God," 256.

77. Ibid., 258.

78. Wiley, *Christian Theology*, 2: 492.

and constant. It is that honorableness of God which secures the creature's hope. It is His boundless, merciful determination to do the creature good. As Collins shows, in Wesley's thought, God expresses holy love in the freely chosen outward movement that stoops down, makes contact and establishes fellowship through the Holy Spirit.[79] Thus, divine holiness drives the invitation to participate in the divine nature and guarantees its actualization. From this perspective, one can clearly see that divine holiness is the bedrock of holiness theology.

As such, the communion paradigm demonstrates the trinitarian basis of entire sanctification, since this experience is the threshold of fullness in fellowship with the triune God. In brief, "relational fullness is the work of the Spirit, who places humans 'in Christ' and thereby effects human participation in the dynamic of the divine life."[80] This perspective has remained latent in holiness theology due to the anthropocentric approach, but becomes evident by considering holiness theology in terms of divine-human participation. For Bresee, entire sanctification is the full actualization, to the believer, of God's desire for fellowship. The work of the Holy Spirit is to purify the heart, illumine the word of God and reveal Christ in the heart of the believer.[81] Wesley asserts that the knowledge of the Blessed Trinity arises in happy and holy communion with God the Father, Son and Holy Ghost.[82] Thus, as Dorr observes, for Wesley, the Holy Spirit effects intimacy between the believer and the three persons of the Trinity.[83] Similarly, Charles M. Wood comments that, for Wesley, the Father reveals the Son through the Holy Spirit.[84] Reflection from the perspective of communion affirms this trinitarian basis for holiness theology.

By extending reflection to the divine life, the communion model allows us to consider human holiness within the framework of divine holiness. It understands human holiness as a possibility and necessity because of divine holiness, expressed in the mercy that makes us partakers of the divine nature, and the power that delivers us from sin.

---

79. Collins, *Holy Love*, 21.

80. Grenz, "The Social God and the Relational Self," 98.

81. "Victory Day," "After Pentecost" (May 31, 1903), "After Pentecost" (June 7, 1903), "To Know Him."

82. "Spiritual Worship," *Works* VI: 432.

83. Dorr, "Wesley's Teaching on the Nature of Holiness," 234.

84. Wood, "Methodist Doctrine," 177–78.

Grace and Reciprocity

Consideration of the *ordo salutis* in terms of communion underscores both divine grace and genuine reciprocity. The divine overture is the basis of divine-human fellowship. Every moment of fellowship with God is due to His gracious approach. The guarantee of fellowship does not limit divine freedom. Instead, God draws near to the creature because He is gracious, merciful and holy. Included in the gracious work of the Spirit is the enablement of human response. Even as the divine approach is free, so is the human response, since, while He enables response, it is the believer who must respond, and this response takes practical form in obedience. The synergy of divine approach and grace-empowered human response sets up a salvific continuum of genuine reciprocity, the basis of which is grace. In sum, the communion model affirms the priority of grace, and moral responsibility as a possibility of grace. Considering the *ordo salutis* as genuine reciprocity attributes appropriate significance to both divine overture and human response without over-valuing the human role, or diminishing divine grace.

Participation and Holiness

By our participation in God, we become like Him. Thus, becoming holy is the outcome of fellowship with God from the moment of the new birth.

Holiness is a mark of participation in God. It is the outcome of the indwelling presence of God.[85] As Bresee states, "The Bible insists upon, and we must have holiness of heart, but we cannot trust in a holy heart; we can trust only in he who dwells within it."[86] Holiness "is the result of the soul's vision of God."[87] In fellowship with God, the human partner is shaped in the divine perfections.[88] This transformation is both inward and outward. Inwardly, holiness is "the image of God stamped upon the heart." Outwardly, holiness is the concrete expression of "continual, thankful love to God as well as love for one another."[89] In sum, holiness is the outcome of participation in God. It is not a once-for-all impartation;

85. Wiley, *Christian Theology*, 2: 492.
86. "Divine Power."
87. "The Motive to Endurance."
88. Charry, "Divine Perfections," 142.
89. "New Birth," *Works* VI: 71.

instead, it is the fruit of moment by moment fellowship with God through the presence of the Holy Spirit.

On this view, there is not a one-to-one correspondence between entire sanctification and holiness. Instead, holiness begins at the new birth when the believer enters into fellowship with God. The Holy Spirit begins to impart holiness in the new birth by deliverance from sin, but also by His indwelling presence. The believer becomes more and more like God as fellowship progresses. Viewing human holiness as an effect of divine-human indwelling avoids elevating one aspect of the salvific continuum over others. This standpoint prevents dissociation of entire sanctification from justification and gradual sanctification. Instead, participation in God begins in justification and, as communion deepens, the believer grows in holiness through the ongoing sanctifying work of the Holy Spirit. In entire sanctification, the Holy Spirit establishes His sole Lordship in the believer's heart. From this point onwards, the rulership of the Holy Spirit enables the believer to be fully receptive to His transforming influence.

It may be argued that the communion paradigm obscures the importance of the second work of grace. However, participation in God throws light on the remaining sinful nature and its antagonism to divine holiness and love. Entire sanctification is an essential element of the salvific continuum because it is deliverance from this antagonistic force. The communion model affirms the importance of this experience by showing that deepening intimacy with God brings the believer into entire sanctification. As the believer grows in faith and the knowledge of God, the Holy Spirit brings awareness of inherited sin, enables repentance, and gives faith for deliverance. As such, the experience can be considered a necessary and possible step in a thriving relationship with God.

Crisis and Process

The reciprocity that moves the *ordo salutis* forward suggests a necessary crisis-process relation. Reciprocity requires discrete responses to the Holy Spirit through decisive obedience. In a sense, reciprocity is a crisis-process relation in which a crisis or decisive moment moves the relationship forward. Clearly, crisis and process are more than just formal elements of religious experience. Instead, they are intrinsic to the faith synergy. This means that the Wesleyan *ordo salutis* requires both crisis and process for coherence. Fundamentally, entire sanctification is one of a series of moments of obedient response to the Holy Spirit that draw the believer into deeper fellowship with God. It is, however, of momentous significance, since it carries the particularity of deliverance from sin and the advent of fullness of communion. Accordingly, entire sanctification may be understood as a moment of significant, qualitative change in divine-human fellowship, preceded and followed by small, discrete, but decisive responses to the Holy Spirit that have the cumulative effect of a process.

Fullness of Communion

Finally, as shown in the thought of both Wesley and Bresee, fellowship with God reaches fullness. In Wesley's construal, fullness of communion refers to the believer's wholehearted love and obedience to the indwelling Holy Spirit. This is a relationship of true oneness with Christ. For Bresee, entire sanctification commences intimate union with Christ, which is the enthronement of Christ as Lord in the believer's life. It is participation in Christ's suffering and resurrection, as well as in His vision of reality. Thus, the qualitative difference in the divine-human relationship that comes through the baptism with the Holy Spirit is that the believer's stance becomes one of complete loyalty and devotion to Christ. The common viewpoint is that fullness of communion refers to the actualization of divine lordship in the believer's life.

On this view, the purpose of entire sanctification is to establish this full lordship. This brings to light the distinction between justification and entire sanctification. It also indicates the necessity of entire sanctification. The rationale for holiness theology is that fullness of communion is a biblical command and promise, and that this quality of relationship is only possible through deliverance from inherited sin. For Wesley, inherited sin is a principle of unbelief, which stands in contradiction to fullness of communion. For Bresee, inherited sin prevents the believer's full conformity to Christ. Cleansing from inherited sin delivers the believer from opposition to the Lordship of Christ and frees the believer for complete receptivity to the Holy Spirit.

Summation

Since the goal of entire sanctification is fullness of communion with God, communion with God underwrites the possibility and necessity of entire sanctification. Fullness of communion requires entire sanctification, an experience that draws the believer into wholehearted participation in the divine fellowship of holy love. This interrelation highlights divine initiative and Lordship, as the principal elements of entire sanctification. Conceiving entire sanctification as an element of the *ordo salutis*, integrates the experience into the wider scope of salvific grace, objectively grounded in Jesus Christ and subjectively actualized through the Holy Spirit. As such, the communion model affirms the preeminence of *sola fide sola gratia*. Moreover, understanding entire sanctification as the threshold into fullness of communion allows us to see the *ordo salutis* as a trajectory of genuine reciprocity drawn forward by grace and faith, crisis and process.

The communion paradigm offers the possibility of developing a holiness theology that imparts distinctive theological identity to the Wesleyan-Holiness tradition, without thereby diminishing the place of other doctrines. Favoring holiness theology over other doctrines may not be the best way to affirm its importance. Bassett observes that this approach affects the whole theological system.[90] In the communion paradigm, the significance of holiness theology is not due to attributing to it greater significance than other doctrines, but rather, expanding its relevance and by disclosing it place within and connection to the whole doctrinal system.

The Ethical Paradigm

In recent decades, one approach to holiness theology has been in terms of perfectioning or virtue formation, an understanding of sanctification as a process of acquiring Christian virtues through emulation of Jesus Christ.[91] I refer to this approach as the ethical paradigm. This section shows that the ethical paradigm addresses the pursuit of perfection, and as such, does not break out of the self-referential framework. On the other hand, the communion model offers the possibility of resolving the tensions that currently attend holiness theology, by expanding its relevance beyond the sphere of moral theology.

90. Bassett, "The Interplay of Christology and Ecclesiology," 79.

91. In addition to Dunning's explication, treated in this section, see also Oord, "Attaining Perfection," 67–68.

Features of the Ethical Paradigm

The proposal of H. Ray Dunning allows us to explore the main features of the ethical paradigm. It defines sanctification as a process of moral transformation through right choices, with the assistance of the Holy Spirit. The thrust of the argument is that explication of entire sanctification must adjust to the ways in which the experience actually happens.[92]

Dunning contends that nineteenth-century holiness theology associated entire sanctification with a single form by enforcing the idea of a second crisis experience as a norm for all believers.[93] Frontier revivalism influenced the propagation of entire sanctification as a crisis experience. Thus, crisis expressed the cultural ethos of revivalism rather than the theological content of entire sanctification. In short, talk about a crisis moment of cleansing from inherited sin is a culturally conditioned notion that is unnecessary to the content of holiness doctrine. In addition, authority for the propagation of entire sanctification shifted from Scripture to experience in the crisis form. This was a reaction to the rising influence of historical criticism in Europe, as well as the revolutionary theories of Sigmund Freud, John Dewey and others. These radical changes led the Movement to view intellectual endeavor with suspicion. Instead, it turned to religious experience and personal testimony as sources of theology.

The rationale for proposing an alternative construal is that emotional crisis is neither necessary to the content of holiness teaching, nor is it an adequate form for the contemporary cultural situation. As such, there is no reason to teach entire sanctification as a crisis experience. He states, "When experience does not support the hypothesis, then it is changed to conform more closely to reality, not vice versa."[94]

Two aspects of Wesley's thought inform the ethical model. First, according to Dunning, Wesley's hermeneutical key is love, understood as ethical choice. He sees Wesley's emphasis on personal transformation as a direct correlation between sanctification and moral responsibility, resulting in empirically verifiable change.[95] In short, for Dunning, Wesley's understanding of sanctification is that it is change in behavior. He contrasts this interpretation of Wesley with the cleansing emphasis in entire sanctification. He argues that the Holiness Movement introduced a cultic or

92. Dunning, "Toward a New Paradigm," 155–56.

93. Ibid., 154.

94. Ibid., 156.

95. Ibid., 157.

ceremonial understanding of cleansing by teaching a religious experience of heart purification, which obscures the importance of moral responsibility, a concept integral to Wesley's view of sanctification. Second, Dunning understands Wesley to mean that Christian perfection is a matter of choosing to be motivated by love. This means that when less-than-perfect motivations arise, the believer ought to "will that they not be present."[96] His interpretation of Wesley's Christian perfection is that the believer is responsible for and capable of making choices in harmony with perfect love.

The basic elements of human character are perceptions, intentions, and dispositions.[97] Perceptions refer to the data arising from one's relation to the perceived world. This provides the subject matter that shapes character. Thus, for example, the subject matter for the Christian is the person of Christ. Intentions are goal-oriented determinations that provide coherence to decisions and actions. Dispositions are the habits of heart and mind, persistent attitudes that are demonstrated in one's behavior. As such, perceptions inform and shape intentions. Consistency in intentions shapes dispositions.

Perfection is the ongoing pursuit of right intentionality, which is an act of will. Sanctification is the ongoing process of choosing good intentions and rejecting unworthy ones. Eventually the believer is able to function consistently with pure intentionality. In this model, perfection is an ongoing pursuit in which one chooses pure intentions as the basis of action. As such, sanctification never becomes "entire" nor does it need to be. Pure intentionality does not mean that wrong intentions do not present themselves. Instead, wrong intentions must be rejected by an act of will. On this view, the function of sanctifying grace is to enable this motion of the will. Dunning is "not suggesting a psychological reorientation merely, but a controlling focus that can only occur when enabled by Divine assistance and then functions in the realm of the moral rather than the magical."[98] In sum, Christian perfection is the development of Christian virtues.

Concerns with the Ethical Paradigm

Dunning identifies key concerns regarding holiness theology: He points out the over-valuation of crisis as a problem in the nineteenth-century

---

96. Ibid., 158–59.
97. Ibid., 159–60.
98. Ibid., 163.

propagation of holiness theology, as well as the need to distinguish between form and content in theological method. His emphasis on the relation between character transformation and sanctification reinforces the practical implications of fellowship with God as well as ethical responsibility. Nonetheless, the ethical model raises concerns in the areas of intentionality and holiness, human agency in sanctification, cleansing from inherited sin and the crisis-process relation.

First, the ethical model seems to indicate a one-to-one correspondence between human intentionality and holiness. Dunning seems to suggest that holiness is right intentionality, and that one has both awareness of and mastery over one's intentions. The implication is that holiness is an action of the will, since intentions can be accepted or refused. If holiness is right intentionally and the latter is an act of will, holiness may be construed as a human work, albeit a work enabled by grace. The concern with this approach is that it dissociates human holiness from life in God. Although relationship with Jesus Christ influences character formation, the model does not fully explain how perfection finds its ground in this relationship. The understanding of this relation is that Jesus presents a pattern to be emulated. This can only be one aspect of the existential significance of Jesus Christ to his followers. A complete explanation of this relation would need to include a fundamental, grace-imparted desire and empowerment to follow Christ as Lord. Thus, the ethical model lacks an adequate theological account of human holiness and this, particularly in relation to divine holiness.

Second, the ethical model seems to over-value human agency in sanctification. The model proposes that the believer can refuse to be motivated by various ungodly impulses by an act of will because of a determining intention to pursue perfection. But this does not explain the source of intentions. Is the individual capable of changing intentions by an act of will? In addition, it should not be presupposed that one is necessarily aware of the intentions that determine choices. The ethical model seems to presuppose precisely this, as well as the volitional capacity to choose intentions. On this view, the role of the Holy Spirit in sanctification is nebulous.

Third, the ethical model suggests that cleansing from sin is a cultic conception that diminishes the importance of moral responsibility. Dunning argues that the Holiness Movement's stress on the cleansing metaphor led to a magical rather than an ethically transformative view of entire sanctification. However, Johnson demonstrates that cleansing is a predominant motif in the New Testament as well as in Wesley, and in neither case does this lead to a magical understanding of sanctification.[99] As shown earlier, for Wesley, cleansing from inherited sin precedes purity of intention. Furthermore, the claim that the cleansing metaphor introduces a cultic perspective in holiness teaching can only be supported if the entirely sanctified do not demonstrate ethical transformation. In addition, an understanding of crisis as cultic or magical seems to preempt the possibility of supernatural action by the Holy Spirit. By eliminating the cleansing work of entire sanctification, the ethical model does not adequately account for pure intentionality.

Furthermore, the model does not fully consider the problem of sin, specifically, inherited sin. Yet, Dunning elsewhere defines the essence of sin as unbelief, pride, disobedience and sensuality,[100] and describes original sin as corruption of nature.[101] He defines humanity's sinful state of being as a lost relation to God.[102] Thus, there needs to be an account of the transformation from a sinful state of being into the image of God, if not by a cleansing experience. Moreover, cleansing from sin would be necessary for the ethical model to be a practical possibility. In the ethical model, "intention builds upon free choice and thus provides a basis for ethical accountability."[103] Simply put, perfection arises as the believer chooses right intentions. We know what right intentions are by examining the life of Jesus. The Holy Spirit gives us the power to choose right intentions. While this approach affirms moral responsibility, it obscures the necessity of grace. The practical result of sin is human incapacity to be oriented to God, which cannot be corrected by an act of will.

Fourth, Dunning eliminates the crisis of entire sanctification because he understands it to be a culturally conditioned form of religious experience that does not resonate with contemporary cultural ethos. However, Wesley taught crisis not as a matter of form, but of content. As shown earlier, entire sanctification is by faith, and for Wesley, this means that the experience occurs at the moment of faith, that is, instantaneously. The ethical model seems to bypass Wesley's theological argument for instantaneity. In fact, the model suggests that Wesley did not teach a crisis experience. As shown earlier, this is not the case. Furthermore,

99. Johnson, "Crisis and Con-Sequence," 190.

100. Dunning, *Grace, Faith and Holiness*, 286.

101. Ibid., 294–95.

102. Ibid., 296–97.

103. Dunning, "Toward a New Paradigm," 160.

the model does not offer an alternative explanation for deliverance from inherited sin. The result is the eclipse of the teaching of a deliverance from inherited sin by grace through faith. This suggests a radical revision of Wesleyan soteriology.

The Possibilities of the Communion Paradigm

The concerns addressed in the ethical model are moral responsibility, cleansing and crisis with respect to entire sanctification. How does the communion paradigm treat these aspects of holiness theology? First, in the communion paradigm, moral responsibility arises from the believer's fellowship with God. Second, the communion model affirms the importance of cleansing from inherited sin as the basis for fullness of communion. Third, it affirms crisis as an element of the theological content of holiness theology.

In the communion paradigm, the capacity for moral responsibility is an element of the Holy Spirit's saving and sanctifying grace. The capacity for right choices comes through fellowship with God. As Johnson points out, "The central idea of Wesleyanism is not the conscious intentionality of love, but the cleansing from sin that pervades the spirit beyond the level of intentionality."[104] Entire sanctification cleanses away the principle of unbelief, self-will and idolatry. Ongoing fellowship through the Holy Spirit's indwelling produces right intentions, and empowers moral choices. Therefore, the model does not disregard moral responsibility, but rather, grounds its possibility in divine grace.

The communion model proposes that fullness of communion requires cleansing from inherited sin. The believer must be freed for intimate union with Christ. It also suggests that there is an underlying corrupt human nature that resists the believer's desire to please God. Pure intention is a result of deliverance from this corruption. This explanation accounts for intentionality, and provides a sound theological basis for ethical transformation.

In the communion model, entire sanctification is an instantaneous experience that ushers in a qualitative change in the divine-human relationship. The communion model understands both regeneration and entire sanctification as threshold experiences that actualize a qualitative change in the divine-human relation. It belongs to the nature of change

104. Johnson, "Crisis and Con-Sequence," 188.

to reach a point of completion. While it is not desirable to over-value the crisis aspect of the Holy Spirit's salvific work, the correction of this problem does not entail eliminating crises in doctrinal formulation. As shown earlier, the communion model overcomes the over-valuation of crisis by explicitly connecting entire sanctification to the Wesleyan *ordo salutis*. Crisis is fundamental to the *ordo salutis* as an aspect of theological content, rather than experiential form.

The communion paradigm seeks to extend the sphere of reflection in holiness theology beyond the transformative effect of entire sanctification in the life of the believer. The standpoint of fullness of communion brings into view the wider soteriological framework as well as the divine nature of holy love. Within this larger sphere, the primacy of grace is clearly visible. Reflection begins with the divine condescension and moves to the salvific mission that draws believers into union with God. This reflection affirms moral responsibility as a possibility and necessity.

Conclusion

This chapter has shown that, for both Wesley and Bresee, the transcendent goal of entire sanctification is fellowship with God. Wesley understands salvation as a dialogue of grace and faith, divine approach and human response. Faith is the God-given capacity for participatory knowledge of God. Fellowship with God begins in the new birth and continues to develop by faith. Cleansing from inherited sin in entire sanctification frees the believer for fullness of communion. In Bresee's thought, full fellowship with God begins with the baptism with the Holy Spirit, which is the revelation of God to the soul, through cleansing from inherited sin and the fullness of the Holy Spirit's indwelling. In sum, for both Wesley and Bresee, there is a point of complete actualization of divine lordship in the believer's heart subsequent to justification, such that the believer can respond to God with complete devotion and allegiance. The term suggested for this qualitative change in divine-human fellowship is fullness of communion. The communion motif brings to light the common underlying theme of both strands—Wesleyan and Holiness—of holiness teaching.

The idea of fullness of communion as the transcendent goal of entire sanctification has provided a starting point for developing the communion paradigm. This orientation draws attention to the divine fellowship of holy love and the astonishing grace that draws us into this fellowship.

The ground of entire sanctification is the very nature of God—holy love expressed in His self-revelation, objectively in Jesus Christ, and in the believer's heart, through the Holy Spirit. This relation affirms that the Holy Spirit's indwelling is an expression of divine grace. This grace makes moral responsibility possible and necessary. Holiness is as the outcome of fellowship with God, which is necessarily transformative. The interconnection of crisis and process is necessary for relationality. Fullness of communion is the kind of fellowship that requires the experience of entire sanctification. These propositions outline the parameters of reflection in the communion model. Clearly, this approach frees holiness theology from subjectivism while safeguarding its experiential character. It extends the sphere of reflection beyond personal religious experience, and suggests a wider definition of holiness theology.

4

The Primacy of Grace

The Dynamics of Entire Sanctification

Introduction

THE QUESTION OF THIS chapter is, "What is the *content* of the experience of entire sanctification construed in terms of participation in God?" I argue that entire sanctification is a decisive moment of faith in which the Holy Spirit cleanses the believer from inherited sin and establishes His complete Lordship through the Gift of His self-outpouring, thereby effecting the believer's full self-giving. The *ordo salutis* is the experiential and theological context of entire sanctification. This experience is a decisive appropriation of grace through faith, in which the Holy Spirit imparts His fullness, thereby expelling the sin principle. The transformative effect of this experience is that it initializes fullness of communion, which is a relationship of wholehearted love and undivided loyalty to God, and a new capacity to love one's neighbor. The first section of this chapter shows that the soteriological context of entire sanctification is a sphere of deepening knowledge of God. The second section shows that sin is a pervasive principle of unbelief and idolatry that determines human disposition and intentionality. The third section demonstrates that the experience of entire sanctification includes repentance and faith, cleansing from inbred sin through divine self-giving, and reciprocal human self-giving. The final section indicates that inward and outward moral transformation is the effect of participation in God through crisis and process interactions. This chapter is an explication of entire sanctification that aims to be theocentric and experiential.

Faith, Grace, and the Knowledge of God

Chapter 2 discussed the Wesleyan *ordo salutis* as the context of entire sanctification and Christian perfection. Chapter 3 illuminated the *ordo salutis* in terms of participation in God, which reaches fullness through entire sanctification. This section builds upon these earlier discussions to underscore that an experiential faith is the conceptual key of the communion model. The concept of faith illuminates the reciprocity of the salvific continuum, as well as the preeminence of grace. By faith comes the knowledge of God that brings the believer into entire sanctification.

Faith

Faith is the appropriate starting point for a Wesleyan theology of holiness because it is the conceptual key of the *ordo salutis*. It is sometimes argued that love is the core principle of Wesley's thought, and should therefore function as the locus of reflection in holiness theology.[1] Indeed, as shown in chapter 2, Wesley's primary interest is heart religion, or pure love for God and one's neighbor. But for Wesley, we love God because He first loved us and because we have come to know that love in a personally meaningful way. This knowledge of God's love, that is, personal awareness and appropriation of God's love, is faith. It initiates and sustains genuine reciprocity between God and the believer. Thus, while the content of heart religion is love, the basis of heart religion is faith.

A Wesleyan concept of faith is inherently experiential. Chapter 2 described Wesley's view of faith as a complex of intellectual assent, trust and personal experience. Faith is God-given certitude about the reality and character of God and His salvation (Heb 11:2; 6; Eph 2:9). Certitude is both cognitive and experiential. It is intellectual assent to as well as inward conviction of truth, which the Holy Spirit imparts (John 16:8–15). Certitude refers to a personal or experiential mode of knowing. It is a perception of the truth as existentially meaningful, and as such, presents the truth as an occasion for trust. While God imparts certitude, the believer is commanded to trust God because He has shown Himself

1. See for example, Wynkoop, *Theology of Love.*

to be worthy of trust (Isa 26:4). By trust, the believer appropriates the knowledge of God. Thus, faith is a knowledge-interaction between God and the believer in which God imparts profound certitude of His trust-worthiness and the believer responds with trust.

Faith is experiential not only because it entails trustful acceptance of what God makes known by His Spirit, but also because faith includes power to act. Spirit-imparted certitude of truth changes one's vision of reality and therefore opens up new choices. Conviction of and trust in the truth mean that the truth determines choices. Thus, the exercise of faith is decisive action in accordance to the knowledge of faith. Acting upon the knowledge of faith opens up the way for more knowledge. While faith itself is a gift of grace, the exercise of faith is an act of will.[2] Thus, as Wesley asserts, "To use all the faith you have will bring an increase of faith."[3] Increasing faith-capacity correlates with increasing knowledge of God. This relation shows that God grants the human partner the privilege and responsibility of engaging in a genuine relationship with Himself. It follows that the experiential concept of faith is the basis for a relational and dynamic *ordo salutis*.

Obedience is the exercise of faith through the principal forms of repentance and love. Obedience is "a faith-response to God's grace-initiative."[4] The knowledge of faith that leads to repentance is the Spirit-imparted certitude of one's sinfulness as well as the divine wrath incurred by sin.[5] Repentance is the human response of obedience to the knowledge revealed by the Holy Spirit.[6] The unbeliever repents by forsaking a life of sin. In the believer's experience, growth in the knowledge of God brings awareness of the divine nature of holiness and love, which fosters humility and repentance, aspects of gradual sanctification. Divine holiness reveals

---

2. Failure to make this distinction has led to a volitional concept of faith. As discussed in chapter 2 this was a significant issue in the nineteenth-century Holiness Movement. As Brindlinger observes, the idea of faith as a human work continues to obscure the giftedness of faith in the holiness strand of evangelicalism. He states, "A widespread misunderstanding of faith among evangelicals, especially evangelicals from the holiness tradition, has to do with HOW we experience faith. They are clear that it is only by faith, not human effort that we come into relationship with God. But then their understanding grows fuzzy. They feel that faith is the result of human effort" (Brindlinger, "Transformative Dimensions," 121).

3. "Letter to a Member (September 15, 1770)," *Works* XII: 288.

4. Rakestraw, "Theologian of Grace," 200.

5. Wiley, *Christian Theology*, 2: 361–62.

6. Ibid., 364.

inbred sin as an obstacle to full fellowship with God. Entire sanctification liberates the believer from this obstacle. Subsequent to entire sanctification, the occasion for the believer's repentance is continued awareness of human weaknesses that impedes the full expression of holiness and love. Thus, the life of faith moves forward in closer fellowship with God as the believer exercises faith through repentance. The second principal form of obedience is love for others. The believer can love because of the certitude of God's love. As faith increases, so does the capacity to love. Increasing trust in God frees the believer from the self-orientation and self-lordship that impede pure love.

Disobedience puts the believer "in danger of forfeiting the favor of God" since it constitutes deliberate rejection of God's grace.[7] Put differently, "faith is that which men possess only insofar as it is that which they do."[8] The whole person must accept the knowledge of the gospel and act accordingly. On this view, the *ordo salutis* is a series of faith decisions through which the believer advances in the knowledge of God by making choices that reflect appropriation of truth.

To summarize, faith is a gift of divine grace that elicits the trust-response of obedience within the framework of grace. As such, God reaches out, saves, cleanses, and draws the human partner into fellowship by grace alone, and faith alone. Faith is an expression of grace by its sheer giftedness, and by its accompanying enablement for human exercise of faith. Only this mutuality can be properly understood as communion. The dignity of personal choice granted to the human partner does not obscure, but rather, illuminates grace. As such, the experiential, interactive concept of faith highlights the nature of salvation as the knowledge of God.

The Preeminence of Grace

The ground for the precedence of grace in the *ordo salutis* is that the whole work of salvation is by grace alone. Divine grace is the unmerited favor whereby God draws human partners into fellowship with Himself through the salvific work of Jesus Christ and the power, presence and action of the Holy Spirit.

The revelation of God in Jesus Christ and the salvation secured for the creation through His blood are the objective ground of all grace talk

---

7. Rakestraw, "Theologian of Grace," 200.

8. Purkiser, Taylor, and Taylor, *God, Man and Salvation*, 419.

in Christian experience. As stated in Rom 5:6, while we were still without strength to think, will, or do anything good Christ died for the ungodly.[9] "The source of the Christian's confidence for the future is the unprecedented, unparalleled demonstration of God's love for us objectively revealed in the death of Christ."[10] Grace is fundamentally the unmerited favor of God in freely reaching out to humanity. The eternal life of the triune God is the ground for this outward movement that expresses His love, freedom and holiness.[11] Thus, grace is free divine self-expression, and as Wiley remarks, the absolute holiness of God expressed in the form of sacrificial love determines the nature of this grace.[12] Therefore, the divine-human communion of the *ordo salutis* can only be considered by virtue and in light of the work of Jesus Christ. It follows that divine unmerited favor underwrites the mutuality of faith and grace which characterizes the existential locus of salvation in the *ordo salutis*.

Grace is the cause of divine-human fellowship. Salvation is "the entire work of God, from the first dawning of grace in the soul, till it is consummated in glory."[13] The Holy Spirit is the efficient cause of all the benefits which come to us through the work of Christ.[14] The Holy Spirit makes us partakers of the divine nature, imparts the sense of belonging to Christ and

---

9. Wesley, *Explanatory Notes Upon the New Testament*, 374.

10. Greathouse and Lyons, *Romans 1–8*, 157–58.

11. 1 Peter 1:20 indicates the free divine determination to save humanity through Jesus Christ, apart from human endeavor. Grace is therefore primarily proactive rather than reactive. Regarding John 1:9, Wesley remarks that Jesus Christ lights every one through what is "vulgarly termed natural conscience, pointing out at least the general lines of good and evil. And this light, if man did not hinder, would shine more and more to the perfect day." Therefore, divine initiative is also evident in the arena of human response, as the grace which precedes and leads to salvation (Wesley, *Explanatory Notes Upon the New Testament*, 213). In "Salvation by Faith" Wesley insists, "All the blessings which God hath bestowed upon man are of his mere grace, bounty, or favour; his free, undeserved favour; favour altogether undeserved; man having no claim to the least of his mercies. It was free grace that 'formed man of the dust of the ground, and breathed into him a living soul,' and stamped on that soul the image of God, and 'put all things under his feet.' The same free grace continues to us, at this day, life, and breath, and all things. For there is nothing we are, or have, or do, which can deserve the least thing at God's hand. 'All our works, Thou, O God, hast wrought in us.' These, therefore, are so many more instances of free mercy: and whatever righteousness may be found in man, this is also the gift of God" (*Works* V: 7).

12. Wiley, *Christian Theology*, 2: 345.

13. "Scripture Way," *Works* VI: 44.

14. Wesley, *Explanatory Notes Upon the New Testament*, 374.

the assurance of eternal happiness.[15] He unites us to Christ and brings us to "a full and eternal enjoyment of God."[16] God's grace is the active presence and power of God in the divine-human relationship.[17] The gracious activity of the Holy Spirit finds its source in God's very being, in His unmerited mercy.[18] Divine grace is entirely independent of human possibility. Instead, it creates all human possibility for fellowship with God. Reflection on the divine initiative illuminates the priority of divine grace.

The Holy Spirit is the administrator of the redemption secured by Jesus Christ.[19] The Holy Spirit actualizes God's unmerited favor in seeking the human partner for salvific fellowship. The first approach of the Holy Spirit is through prevenient grace. This is the source of all human movement towards God, through the drawing of the Holy Spirit, and conscience.[20] Prevenient grace awakens "the soul to the truth upon which religion rests," and moves "upon the affections by enlisting the heart upon the side of truth."[21] "Prevenient grace provides . . . the incentive to follow the good, the knowledge of the good and even the power to choose for the good."[22] In sum, the prevenient work of the Holy Spirit imparts the beginning of spiritual life which leads on to further life as the individual responds to grace. In this sense, every person has a degree of divine life, and a real capacity to choose God, not as a birthright, but by grace.[23] Thus, while grace is sovereign, it is not irresistible—it enables rather than overrides human will. It "enables forgiven sinners to live in obedience and honor God with their transformed lives."[24] The God-given empowerment to respond ascribes dignity to the human partner, since it opens up the possibility of creaturely engagement in genuine fellowship with the Creator.

The unmerited favor of God surrounds the synergy of divine action and human response. Its objective ground is the work of Christ, which is itself a free action of grace.[25] The synergistic paradigm of divine

15. "Grieving the Holy Spirit," *Works* VII: 492.

16. "Letter to a Roman Catholic," *Works* X: 82.

17. Heitzenrater, "God with Us," 92.

18. "Working out our Own Salvation," *Works* VI: 508.

19. Wiley, *Christian Theology*, 2: 303.

20. "Scripture Way," *Works* VI: 44.

21. Wiley, *Christian Theology*, 2: 357.

22. Cox, "Prevenient Grace," 147.

23. Ibid.

24. Greathouse and Lyons, *Romans 1–8*, 177–78.

25. Collins identifies two problems which attend limiting divine grace to the

and human acting finds its basis in the sole activity of God.[26] "Thus, the grace of God ever precedes us, demonstrating once again the favor and goodness of the Most High, as well as, in this context, the empowerment and imperative that such grace affords."[27] Reduction of grace to the faith-grace synergy means that "once the initial or prevenient action of the Most High occurs, then God is virtually limited to responding merely to human response."[28] Divine grace must be understood as primarily free, and only in this freedom does cooperant grace arise as a possibility. If salvation "were understood apart from the outgoing love of God that ever seeks fellowship and communion, then it could easily become the bricks and mortar of an all-too-human, dour religion in which the purpose of fellowship and community, the love of God and neighbor, would easily be lost in self-preoccupation and spiritual narcissism."[29] Put differently, reduction of God's grace to the synergistic mode results in over-valuation of human agency in salvation.

In sum, the primacy of grace is visible in the free self-disclosure of God in Jesus Christ, as well as in the divine approach and engagement with the human partner in fellowship through the Holy Spirit. Therefore, affirmation of the primacy of grace shows the trinitarian basis of the Wesleyan *ordo salutis*. As Wesley insists, what God has done for us in Christ must be done in us through the Holy Spirit.[30] "All grace comes to us from

synergistic paradigm. First, "if divine initiative is presupposed, then the soteriological emphasis may in practice devolve on human initiative and works viewed, of course, as a 'response.' In other words, here the danger of moralism and self justification ever loom." Second, "the ascription of a synergistic model to Wesley's theology might easily suggest an equality of soteriological roles in terms of God and humanity, even though the putative emphasis is on divine prevenient action. More to the point, . . . once divine initiative occurs, God repeatedly and consistently acts only in response to ongoing human response. In other words, the decisiveness of God, the sheer gratuity of grace, as well as the sovereignty of divine action in the face of human impotence, may all be minimized if not repudiated" (Collins, "Recent Trends," 80–88).

26. Collins, *Holy Love*, 12–13.

27. Ibid., 156.

28. Ibid., 164.

29. Ibid., 9.

30. Wesley asserts that religion begins "when we begin to know God, by the teaching of his own Spirit. As soon as the Father of spirits reveals his Son in our hearts, and the Son reveals his Father, the love of God is shed abroad in our hearts." Happiness comes in "constant communion with the Father, and with his Son Jesus Christ; then, in all the heavenly tempers which he hath wrought in us by his Spirit" ("Unity of the Divine Being," *Works* VII: 269–70).

the love of the Father through Jesus Christ and his life, death, resurrection, and ascension, and is mediated to us by the power and presence of the Holy Spirit."[31] Thus, the preeminence of grace draws reflection to the triune fellowship of holy love as the source and goal of salvation.

The Knowledge of God

The discussion thus far in this chapter has shown that experiential faith is the key concept of the Wesleyan *ordo salutis*, and that grace is the cause of participation in God. The dynamic, grace-enabled continuum constitutes increasing knowledge of God and is the locus for entire sanctification.

The content of faith is salvific knowledge of God. First, preliminary knowledge of God comes to all through prevenient grace. Obedient response draws the individual into saving faith, which is the conviction of the saving love of God through Jesus Christ.[32] Saving faith brings the believer into new life in Christ—a sphere of existence by faith, which becomes a permanent attitude.[33] Thus, "One does not exercise faith as an isolated event but begins a walk of faith marked by continuing dependence upon the mercy and grace of God."[34] Saving faith is the condition of justification, which marks the beginning of fellowship with God. Justification is reconciliation of the sinner to God through faith in the merits of Christ.[35] The gracious act of justification is the first threshold moment of the *ordo salutis* and the necessary foundation for fellowship with God because it imparts the conviction of God's loving and gracious acceptance.

Knowledge of God's love effects the transformation that accompanies justification.[36] Thus, in addition to relative change, there is real change.[37]

31. Colyer and Cieslukowski, "Wesley's Trinitarian *Ordo Salutis*," 123.

32. Wiley, *Christian Theology*, 2: 368.

33. Ibid., 375 (Wiley's conclusion is based on Col 2:6–7 and Gal 5:6).

34. Dunning, *Grace, Faith and Holiness*, 440–41.

35. "Scripture Way of Salvation," *Works* VI: 44–45.

36. Knight, "Transformation of the Human Heart," 51–52.

37. Wesley is wary of antinomian interpretations of imputation. To overcome this possibility he makes justification and sanctification inseparable. Thus, according to Bolster ("Wesley's Doctrine of Justification") Wesley's concept of imputation means that "Christ is the Author of our salvation, the One who purchased the benefits of the New Covenant, and whose death is the ground of our forgiveness" (ibid., 149). "Justification and the commencement of sanctification, like pardon and acceptance, are two moments in a total experience, which may be distinguished but not divided. Good works must follow justification as surely as they cannot procure it. A faith that does not produce

The spiritually dead sinner is brought into newness of spiritual life and righteousness.[38] The conversion experience of justification and regeneration "is an encounter with God's love that lays a new foundation relationally and dispositionally, enabling subsequent growth in the Christian life."[39] The new believer becomes a partaker of the divine nature and learns "through experience the kind of a being God is."[40] Accordingly, regeneration marks the beginning of a new sphere of existence, characterized by increasing fellowship with God and concomitant gradual sanctification.

Sanctification is gradual growth in inward and outward holiness from the moment of regeneration.[41] It is the effect of daily increase in the knowledge of God and fellowship with the Father and the Son through the Holy Spirit, which produces "new tastes, new desires and new dispositions."[42] Moreover, the knowledge of God's holiness and love discloses inbred sin and imparts yearning for deliverance. The believer's deepening love for God and awareness of inbred sin as an obstacle to wholehearted love evoke the desire for deliverance.

Consequently, there is a second threshold experience which effects deliverance and fullness of communion. This is the experience of entire sanctification. Parallel to the experience of justification and regeneration, the believer, in a moment of faith, repents of inherited sin and receives the cleansing of the Holy Spirit.[43] Through deliverance from inherited sin, the believer becomes completely receptive to the Holy Spirit so that He assumes full Lordship. He fills the believer to the fullness of the soul's

---

holiness is no faith at all" (ibid., 152). Wiley warns against overstating the relative change of justification (imputation) at the expense of impartation of righteousness, the subjective work of the Spirit (*Christian Theology*, 2: 399). Following Wesley, he asserts first, that imputation must be considered alongside impartation of righteousness. Second, he points out that faith is imputed for righteousness. He reasons that since all who believe are justified (Acts 13:39), and since Abraham's faith was imputed as righteousness (Rom 4:22), faith as a personal act of the believer is imputed for righteousness, so that faith is the condition of righteousness and not itself righteousness. He remarks, "St. Paul insists that faith is the condition of righteousness, and therefore 'of faith' simply means the legal state consequent upon the remission of sins through faith" (ibid., 401).

38. "New Birth," *Works* VI: 71.

39. Knight, "Transformation of the Human Heart," 54.

40. Wiley, *Christian Theology*, 2: 425.

41. "New Birth," *Works* VI: 74.

42. Ibid., 70–71; Wiley, *Christian Theology*, 2: 411.

43. Collins, *Holy Love*, 284.

capacity. The effect of this experience is a qualitative difference in divine-human communion and heart purity.

The *ordo salutis* extends beyond the experience of entire sanctification through continual increase in the knowledge of God. The effect of deepening intimacy with God under the full influence of the Holy Spirit is that the believer pursues a lifestyle in harmony with pure love. The fruit of the Holy Spirit increasingly characterizes the believer's relationships and attitudes. The believer's progress depends on factors such as emotional damage, ingrained sinful habits, personality, and physical weaknesses, which may be more easily overcome by some than by others. This is the ongoing experience of fullness of communion.

Summation

The preceding discussion developed the experiential and theological context of entire sanctification. The experiential concept of faith illuminates grace as the cause of participation in God. Thus, "the experiential exigencies of faith are preeminently grounded in the prior initiative of grace."[44] The knowledge of God is "a lively, personal affair, yet due to God's initiative, not ours. It is fundamentally and eminently *God's* remedy. It must follow, then, that soteriological effects flow from epistemological activity."[45] Accordingly, the knowledge of God effects sanctification and it is this process that moves the divine-human fellowship towards the experience of entire sanctification. This approach is one way to safeguard the teleological character of holiness theology as both crisis and process. As Collins observes, "Once a specific doctrine is located within the Wesleyan order of salvation, it must be expounded with reference to what both precedes and follows it within that theological structure."[46] This approach grounds a particular soteriological focus, such as entire sanctification, in the order of salvation. Furthermore, as Wesley warns, failure to correctly view entire sanctification within the *ordo salutis* overshadows justification by faith.[47] This framework explicitly connects entire sanctifi-

44. Ayers, "John Wesley's Therapeutic Understanding," 277.

45. Ibid., 278.

46. Collins, "A Hermeneutical Model," 25.

47. "Satan's Devices," *Works* VI: 38 (Wesley states that it is a device of Satan to "make void the counsel of God, by dividing the gospel against itself, and making one part of it overthrow the other; while the first work of God in the soul is destroyed by the expectation of his perfect work").

cation to the *ordo salutis* and to divine grace, which is the outflow of the triune fellowship of holy love.

Inbred Sin

The rationale for an *ordo salutis* that includes entire sanctification is that inbred sin remains in the believer and constitutes an obstacle to fullness of communion. This section shows that sin is a pervasive principle of unbelief and idolatry. Sin is not only deprivation of fellowship but is also a profound corruption that necessarily attends deprivation.

Inbred Sin as Deprivation

The deprivation view of sin arises from a relational view of human personhood. According to Wynkoop, the main proponent of this view, to be a person is to love, and one loves by way of the faculties of personality, such as volition, affect, and rationality.[48] This relational anthropology does not construe human personality in terms of a sub-volitional nature, but rather as a communication center designed to love. Thus, persons possess a moral nature which belongs to the rational, conscious self. The moral nature determines the object of love. The result of the Fall is alienation from God and orientation of love to the self.[49]

Since the moral nature belongs to the rational, conscious self, sin belongs in the realm of responsible personhood.[50] For Wynkoop, defining humanness in terms of a sub-volitional nature locates inherited sin outside the sphere of moral responsibility. She explains, "When sin is put outside the rational and responsible nature of man, the thing sin is, is no longer the deadly moral and spiritual force that could occasion all

---

48. Wynkoop, *Theology of Love*. Wynkoop's proposal has been followed by Dunning, *Grace, Faith and Holiness*; Leclerc, *Discovering Christian Holiness*.

49. Wynkoop, *A Theology of Love*, 142.

50. Wynkoop writes, "Wesleyan theology rejects the concept of original holiness as an impersonal goodness, in favor of a more biblical idea of holiness which stresses a right personal relationship to God. Holiness, or morality, is never a quality of impersonal substance but the way one reacts to God and to persons. To understand this is to help correct the idea that sin has substance or is a thing which can be—or cannot be— removed as a diseased part of the body. Holiness is not metaphysically conditioned substance, but a proper relationship to God by the Holy Spirit" (ibid., 177).

that Christ found it necessary to do for mankind."[51] Thus, inherited sin is commitment to a controlling center other than God, and sins are those actions which arise from this commitment. A person is responsible for and aware of sin, or idolatrous commitment. This perversion is inherited by way of a spiritual interconnectedness of human persons that penetrates to the core of humankind.

Since sin is an idolatrous commitment, salvation is the appropriation of grace in order to make a conscious commitment to love God. For Wynkoop, the grace of God "enables a free choice to break away from false allegiance."[52] She contends, "God acts in the only area of man's true freedom and makes decision not only possible and desirable but also mandatory."[53] Thus, the Holy Spirit enables the commitment of one's love to God. Subsequent to justification, love becomes increasingly oriented to God. Entire sanctification marks the moment when one decides to love God alone. On this view, the "entire" in entire sanctification refers to the entirety of one's love-commitment to God. Holiness is the relationship of complete commitment to God. It is "unobstructed personal communion and deep, personal fellowship with God."[54] Thus, sin is orientation of love to the self, while holiness is the orientation of love towards God. As such, sin is absence of fellowship with God, or lack of love for God.

Denial of a sub-volitional human nature leads to the association of inbred sin to human volition. As a consequence, the work of the Spirit is to enable the will to orient love towards God. This view seems to limit the divine role in salvation since it sets human responsibility alongside the divine role. The implication is that the synergistic paradigm is the only realm of God's salvific action. On this view, human choice *entirely* conditions grace. Moreover, the model seems to overlook the Spirit's work in revealing sin. As discussed earlier, Wesley understood both knowledge of sin and human helplessness as integral to the believer's repentance prior to entire sanctification. Furthermore, for Wesley, recognition of one's sin and helplessness is only possible by divine grace. Thus, the relational model views divine grace entirely within the faith-grace synergy of the *ordo salutis*, thereby reducing the action of divine grace to the sphere of divine-human interaction. As Quanstrom observes, the Wynkoop

51. Ibid., 153.
52. Ibid., 159.
53. Ibid., 159.
54. Ibid., 154.

deprivation model is oriented "not so much on the grace of God in the salvation process as on the moral responsibility of persons for their salvation."[55]

The deprivation model does not fully harmonize with Wesley's concept of sin. There are multiple references to "inbred" corruption or corruption of the "inmost nature" throughout the Wesley corpus.[56] Wesley understands sin as a corruption of human nature as a result of loss of fellowship. He states, "Man, in his natural state, is altogether corrupt, through all the faculties of his soul: corrupt in his understanding, his will, his affections, his conscience, and his memory."[57] Wynkoop seems to overlook this aspect of Wesley's thought in her treatment of the sermons, "Sin in Believers" and "The Repentance of Believers."[58] In both of these sermons, the thrust of Wesley's argument is that inbred sin is perversion of love as well as a deep-seated corruption ensuing from absence of fellowship with God. In sum, a person is either a child of God or a child of the devil. For Wesley, only by clearly understanding the human predicament can one come to grips with the cruciality of grace. Furthermore, he understands the fundamental character of sin as lack of knowledge of God since, "we cannot love whom we do not know."[59] This practical atheism must be healed by the gift of faith. Therefore, faith, not love, is the core of Wesley's soteriology, since one loves God by faith and expresses faith by loving others. Undoubtedly, Wesley's concept of inherited sin shows a marked difference from sin in the relational model.

In addition, the deprivation view does not fully account for the biblical description of sin. The weight of Scripture seems to suggest that sin is an inherited principle that controls human knowing and doing. As such, it is a law. According to Rom 8:2, "the law of sin and death" refers to an operative principle in contradiction to the rule of the "law of the Spirit of life."[60] This principle is "self-centeredness, self-will, and self-trust," which cannot be overcome in our own power.[61] The import of these comments

---

55. Quanstrom, *Century of Holiness Theology*, 145.

56. See for example, "Way to the Kingdom," *Works* V: 82 and "Circumcision of the Heart," V: 208.

57. "The Doctrine of Original Sin," *Works* IX: 443.

58. Wynkoop, *Theology of Love*, 153.

59. "Original Sin," *Works* VI: 59.

60. Greathouse and Lyons, *Romans 1–8* (1:8), 228.

61. Ibid., 197.

is that sin, in Pauline thought, refers to a ruling principle that dominates the will, rather than an orientation of the will.

Wynkoop's insistence upon the dynamic nature of holiness, the cruciality of love, and the imperative of moral responsibility resonates with the communion model. The preceding discussion suggests the need for a concept of sin that is appreciative of Wynkoop's dynamic construal, but that also takes into account the element of depravation in the concept of sin, the primacy of grace and the pivotal role of faith in Wesley's thought. In response, the communion paradigm seeks to formulate a concept of sin from the standpoint of salvation by faith.

Inbred Sin: A Pervasive Principle

Whereas the deprivation model describes sin as a wrong orientation of love, the communion model views sin as a pervasive principle of unbelief and idolatry that stands in contradiction to wholehearted love for God. The presupposed anthropology of the communion model is that a person is a relational being whose being transcends its relations. That is to say, there is a "who" that relates.[62] In brief, a relational view of personhood does not negate the idea of a sub-volitional nature or substance.[63] The point of issue here, with regards to holiness theology, is whether there is a corrupt, sub-volitional moral nature that requires cleansing in order to initialize fullness in divine-human fellowship. If sin is a volitional disorder, then there seems to be no rationale for a second work of grace. This disorder can be progressively corrected by way of the salvific synergy of ongoing fellowship with God. On the other hand, if humanity is under the dominion of sin as a ruling principle that controls volition, and which remains subsequent to justification, then this would suggest an *ordo salutis* that includes a second work of grace. I argue that sin is a pervasive principle of enmity to God that determines both the character of persons and their relationships.

Scripture distinguishes between sins as movement of the will, and sin as a sub-volitional pervasive principle. Sins arise in the realm of human knowing and volition. That is, to sin (verb) is to knowingly choose that

---

62. Collins, *Holy Love*, 86.

63. Taylor, *Theological Formulation*, 99–100. Like Taylor, Wood (*Pentecostal Grace*, 163.) and Grabowski ("Person: Substance and Relation," 163.) argue that a relational view of personhood does not require the negation of the concept of substance.

which displeases God. On the other hand, sin (noun) is a ruling principle in human existence. The Roman epistle underscores the idea of sin as a ruling principle. Greathouse explains, "It is noteworthy that *hamartia* appears with the definite article *hē* (lit. 'the sin') no less than twenty-eight times between 5:12 and 8:10, identifying sin as a ruling power and principle, which Christ alone can dethrone by the greater power of the indwelling Holy Spirit." Paul uses the noun *hamartia* to describe "'Sin' as a personified force . . . which rules our human existence . . ."[64] Overall, the Pauline view of the sin principle is that it is a mind-set, an allegiance or a sphere of influence. These descriptions suggest that sin is more than an orientation of the will. It is a deeper determination that orders all the faculties of personality, including the will. On this view, sin is not a "thing" but rather, a systemic moral corruption of being, knowing and doing.

One concern the deprivation model identifies is that viewing sin as a sub-volitional principle denies human responsibility. However, as Wesley asserts, lack of self knowledge is an element of sin.[65] The need for the Spirit's revelation of inbred sin is one indication that sin is a determinative principle beneath the level of human volition and awareness. Awareness of inbred sin only arises as the believer continues to develop in the life of faith through the illumination of the Holy Spirit. Hence, awareness of inherited sin is an element of the knowledge of faith. With awareness comes moral responsibility, since faith requires decisive action in accordance to God-given knowledge. Thus, to speak of the sin principle as a sub-volitional bent in humanity's constitution, is not to deny moral responsibility. Rather, moral responsibility arises as the Holy Spirit reveals the depths of depravity. As such, complete orientation of love to God is only possible as the Holy Spirit both reveals and dissolves inward corruption and the perversion of love, thereby freeing the whole person to love God.

Moral responsibility can only arise as the Holy Spirit graciously reveals the depths of depravity. The determination of the human will to love God is only possible as the Holy Spirit both reveals and corrects the perversion of love.

Furthermore, sin is an inherited way of being. "As a consequence of Adam's sin, every member of the human race has been afflicted with the situation of death—conceived as moral bankruptcy, weakness, and

---

64. Greathouse and Lyons, *Romans 1–8*, 111.

65 "Deceitfulness of Man's Heart," *Works* VII: 341.

corruption."[66] This is not to say that all sinned implicitly in Adam. Instead, "all of Adam's descendants share in the adverse *consequences* of his sin, which extend to the entire human race."[67] In sum, humanity has inherited a type of existence that unwittingly subscribes to a false allegiance.

The impact of this false allegiance, that is, denial of divine lordship, issues in pervasive corruption. As Greathouse states, "deprived of a right relationship with God, all human beings without exception are blind, helpless, and corrupt. They embody what theologians call 'total depravity.' Their character is marked by a steady disposition to rebel against God."[68] Corruption issues in choices that wrong God and one's neighbor, which is due to loss of fellowship with God. Wesley points out, "Adam's change in his relationship to God, which was now a perverted one, affected the tempers of his heart, the seat of holiness and love, tempers that together constituted his basic orientation, his predisposition, toward all thought and action."[69] Inherited sin, then, is a pervasive principle of enmity to God, "an inexhaustible fund of ungodliness and unrighteousness so deeply and strongly rooted in the soul, that nothing less than almighty grace can cure it."[70]

The sin principle remains subsequent to regeneration. In the life of the believer, there are two competing mind-sets. These two mind-sets do not refer to a body-soul dualism, nor is sin to be understood in substantial terms. On the contrary, the same self may ascribe to either the mind-set of Spirit and life, or the mind-set of sin and death.[71] The believer is able to choose the law of the Spirit rather than the law of sin and death. Yet, there remains in the believer that which opposes the lordship of the indwelling Holy Spirit. "Believers have been set free from the power of sin, yet sin remains, although it does not reign. And Christ cannot reign where sin remains. Sin remains as self-centeredness, self-will and self-trust. That sin remains is shown by our obsession with the illusion that we can maintain our new life and freedom on our own, in our own power."[72]

To summarize, sin is a pervasive principle that corrupts human disposition and volition. It is an inherited bent to self-allegiance. In

66. Greathouse and Lyons, *Romans 1–8*, 163.

67. Ibid.

68. Ibid., 112.

69. Collins, *Holy Love*, 63.

70. "Deceitfulness of Man's Heart," *Works* VII: 340.

71. Greathouse and Lyons, *Romans 1–8*, 226.

72. Ibid., 197.

justification, believers are set free from the rulership of sin through the Holy Spirit. Thus, in the life of the believer, sin no longer reigns. Yet, the principle remains, and is an obstacle to full allegiance to Jesus Christ, the rightful Lord. On this view, entire sanctification is necessary for deliverance from sin so that the believer may engage in full relationality with Jesus Christ through the Holy Spirit.

Sin: Unbelief and Idolatry

The nature of the pervasive principle is enmity against God, and in the life of the believer, a powerful enemy of divine-human fellowship. Sin is a complex of unbelief and idolatry that pervades human knowing, being, and doing. This concept of sin is derived from the principle that salvation by faith is a reversal of unbelief for full restoration of communion with God, and full allegiance to divine Lordship, actualized through the Holy Spirit in the life of the believer.

First, inherited sin is a principle of unbelief that pervades human being, knowing and doing. Wesley describes unbelief as "the confluence of all sins."[73] It is the root of evil, and its essence is departure from God.[74] Taylor observes that unbelief is a libel on the integrity of God.[75] Unbelief is lack of knowledge of God, or spiritual blindness.[76] In sum, unbelief is the root of resistance to God. It is a deep turning way to another source of life and help. It is lack of knowledge of God, or failure to recognize God as the only legitimate Lord. Thus, unbelief is in opposition to divine-human fellowship. The presence of inherited sin therefore produces a conflict in the believer's life, since the believer must strive against the principle of unbelief in the quest for the knowledge of God. Although the Holy Spirit enables the believer to overcome in this struggle, unbelief is in opposition to fullness of communion.

Second, sin is a principle of idolatry. To be human is to live under lordship of some kind, a point of reference. As such, turning from God in unbelief means that one must look to the created order for a point of reference. Thus, idolatry is rebellion. Scripture associates unbelief and rebellion. The writer to the Hebrews urges believers to see to it that no one has a

73 Wesley, *Explanatory Notes Upon the New Testament*, 260.

74. Ibid., 570.

75. Taylor, *Theological Formulation*, 63.

76. "Original Sin," *Works* VI: 58.

sinful, unbelieving heart that turns away from the living God like those who hardened their hearts in the day of rebellion. They were not able to enter into the promised rest because of their unbelief (Heb 3:12, 15, 19, paraphrase mine). Sin is here understood as a complex of unbelief, idolatry, disobedience and revolt. Greathouse describes the Pauline view of sin as analogous to a "deadly virus in humanity, a fundamental revolt against the Creator that places the self and its perceived needs in the place that should be only occupied by the sovereign God."[77] Self-will is also a species of idolatry since in essence it is the determination to go one's own way, to establish one's self as the center of existence.[78] This ensues in a profound commitment to self-governance and the pursuit of self-gratification. Idolatry is in opposition to the Lordship of Jesus Christ, and as such, stands in contradiction to fellowship with God, for fellowship with God is only possible to the extent that His lordship is acknowledged. Although the believer does not give way to the indwelling principle of idolatry, the presence of this latter pulls against the believer's desire for the sole rulership of the Holy Spirit. Even as divine-human communion develops by faith, the believer becomes increasingly aware of this contradictory principle.

Summation

Consideration of inherited sin as essentially a principle of unbelief and idolatry connects the sin problem to its solution—salvation by faith. Unbelief is antithetical to the knowledge of God, and faith imparts that knowledge. The fundamental character of sin is opposition to divine grace and lordship. Unbelief produces idolatry in the form of pride and self-will. In essence, idolatry is the replacement of the Creator with created things. Pride and self-will are in contradiction to wholehearted love for God. When inherited sin is understood as a principle of unbelief, both the gravity of sin and the need for divine grace are affirmed without obscuring moral responsibility. Sin is understood as a pervasive principle, beyond the grasp of the human will. In fact, the human will is itself in subjection to it. This affirms the need for grace, because it points to a degree of human helplessness for which there is no rescue outside of grace. Yet, grace restores the capacity for God and gives the knowledge of this inward condition. Therefore, divine grace makes moral responsibility both necessary and possible.

77. Greathouse and Lyons, *Romans 1–8*, 164.
78. "Original Sin," *Works* VI: 60.

The communion model is dynamic and relational, yet it negates neither a transcendent self, nor a morally responsible self.

The Dynamics of Entire Sanctification

The experience of entire sanctification is the moment of repentance, faith, and divine self-giving, which cleanses sin and enables human self-giving. The heart of holiness theology is that entire sanctification frees the believer from this inbred sin and for fullness of communion. This section unfolds the elements of the experience of entire sanctification: it is necessarily a decisive moment of the Spirit's impartation of faith and the believer's trust-response for deliverance from inbred sin. The work of the Spirit is nothing short of a deeper revelation of Christ that expels sin and enables the believer's reciprocal self-giving and complete allegiance to God.

Repentance

Entire sanctification is preceded by repentance, the believer's response to the God-given awareness of inbred sin that arises in communion with God. Chapter 3 showed that Wesley understands the believer's repentance to include conviction of inbred sin, guiltiness before God, and complete helplessness. The believer's repentance is, first, the conviction of inbred sin and the need for divine deliverance. Second, repentance is expressed by seeking deliverance from inbred sin through the means of grace. Third, it is the renunciation of false allegiances. Faith answers this repentance by the personal conviction that God can and does purify the heart.[79]

First, repentance is the conviction of inbred sin. For Wesley, the repentance precedent to entire sanctification is "one kind of self-knowledge, the knowing ourselves sinners, yea, guilty, helpless sinners, even though we know we are children of God."[80] In other words, the Holy Spirit makes the believer aware of the gravity of inward sin. Believers cannot know the deep corruption of their hearts "until God unveils the inbred monster's face, and shows them the real state of their souls."[81] This repentance is necessary "for, till we are sensible of our disease, it admits no cure."[82]

79. "Repentance of Believers," *Works* V: 168.

80. Ibid., 156–70.

81. Ibid., 169.

82. Ibid., 165.

Repentance is the conviction of the presence of inherited sin remaining in the heart, of its opposition to God and of one's personal helplessness to dispense with it.

Second, repentance includes a response to the conviction of inbred sin. The believer must seek deliverance through entire sanctification. For Wesley, one seeks entire sanctification by the works of repentance. These are the works of piety and the works of mercy. The works of piety are prayer, fasting, hearing and reading the Bible, partaking of the Lord's Supper. The works of mercy are acts of service to others to promote their spiritual and physical well-being. For Wesley, this is the God-ordained manner to wait for entire sanctification.[83] Taken from the standpoint of fellowship with God, if one is to continue in fellowship, grace must be appropriated and faith exercised so that fellowship with God is allowed to change one's behavior, dispositions and tempers. This is a description of gradual sanctification or increasing in holiness, which is the effect of growing knowledge of God.

Third, repentance includes recognition and renunciation of false allegiances. False allegiances come to light through the knowledge of God as the one Lord. As the believer grows in the knowledge of God, sin becomes visible in its form of resistance to the lordship of Jesus Christ. The believer grows in the desire for divine lordship, but becomes increasingly aware of a firm, opposing resolve, evidenced by dispositions, affections, and choices. Repentance includes resistance to the impulse of self-lordship. Therefore, it is a mortification of the self, and not a consecration of the self.

Consecration is often considered a prerequisite for entire sanctification but this view is not in harmony with salvation by faith alone. The idea of consecration as a prerequisite of entire sanctification entered holiness theology by way of Phoebe Palmer's teaching. Greathouse remarks that Palmer's "explicit emphasis upon consecration as a prerequisite is a patent departure from Wesley."[84] On the other hand, for Wesley, entire sanctification is by faith alone. To propose consecration as a prerequisite for entire sanctification makes the experience something other than an element of the *ordo salutis*, since it can no longer be considered a possibility by faith alone.

Consecration is a multi-faceted concept that includes an element of repentance. Taylor describes consecration as "the decisive presentation

83. "Scripture Way of Salvation," *Works* VI: 51; Wiley, *Christian Theology*, 2: 482.

84. Greathouse and Bassett, *Historical Development*, 300.

of self to God for sacrifice or service."[85] It includes the idea of devotement, concentration, and death. Devotement refers to deliberately putting one's self entirely at the disposal of God. Concentration refers to a focused attention on only that which directs or flows from one's single interest, Christ. Death refers to the mortification of self, the surrender of one's personal dreams, ambitions and pursuits. Positively, consecration is complete self-giving to God, and negatively, it is self-mortification.

Complete self-giving to God cannot be considered a prerequisite for entire sanctification because this is impossible while inherited sin remains. Entire sanctification *enables* the believer's complete surrender to the Lordship of Jesus Christ through cleansing from inherited sin. As such, consecration, positively understood, is an element of entire sanctification rather than a prerequisite for this work of grace.

On the other hand, in the sense of self-mortification, consecration is an aspect of the believer's repentance. Self-mortification is the renunciation of one's dreams, ambitions and pursuits—in short, renunciation of self-governance. Repentance is the refusal to act according to the principle of idolatry. Even as the Holy Spirit shows the presence and manifestation of this principle, the believer repents and seeks deliverance. This explanation retains the harmony of the entire sanctification experience with salvation by faith, without denying the importance of the believer's responsibility to surrender all false allegiances.

In sum, the believer's repentance is co-incident with gradual sanctification, and these are elements of the knowledge that comes in fellowship with God. The overall effect of fellowship is transformation. Altogether, this is a movement towards the decisive moment of cleansing from sin.

The Decisive Moment

As already shown, from the standpoint of communion, life in the Spirit advances through faith and obedience. Grace enables choices that harmonize with the knowledge of God. One advances in this relationship by a series of decisive moments of faith, or "faith-grasp."[86] Entire sanctification is a unique decisive moment by virtue of the momentous change it initiates in divine-human relation.

---

85. Taylor, *Theological Formulation*, 171.
86. Carver, "'Secondness' of Entire Sanctification," 12.

Although entire sanctification is set within the ongoing decisive moments of life with God, it is unique because it ushers in a qualitative change in divine-human fellowship. As Knight observes, "What is distinctive about an instantaneous work of grace is the nature of the transformation."[87] In entire sanctification, the believer exercises faith in choosing a single basis for existence, a single Lord and renouncing false trust and allegiance. It is a decision to live only according to the Spirit, to ground one's existence and self-expression in the one God, known in fellowship through the Holy Spirit; it is a singular faith in Jesus Christ. Subsequent fullness of communion consists of faith decisions in harmony with this fundamental transfer of allegiances. The kind of decision that it is sets entire sanctification apart from other decisive moments of faith in the life of the believer. Entire sanctification is a crisis experience because the exercise of faith is a decisive act.

Entire sanctification is necessarily an instantaneous actualization of grace. In fellowship with God, there must come a moment when the Spirit's action completely frees the believer from unbelief and idolatry. There must be a point in time when the divine-human relationship moves into wholeheartedness in faith and love. Thus, it is a threshold transformation.[88] Entire sanctification is a crisis experience, not only because it is a decisive exercise of faith, but also because this action of the will arises through a prior, powerful action of grace. Collins affirms, "The instantaneous motif in terms of justification, regeneration, and entire sanctification reveals that it is God, after all, who both forgives sins and makes one holy."[89] Furthermore, because entire sanctification is by faith alone, it is the work of a moment.[90] Collins warns that to stress the process element of the Christian life "to the virtual neglect of the decisive activity of God may result in sinners being told that today is not after all the day of salvation."[91] Therefore, the basis for the instantaneity of entire sanctification is its character as an element of salvation by faith alone through grace alone.

Although entire sanctification is necessarily a decisive moment, it is not necessarily an emotionally charged experience. The critical instant of entire sanctification is one of faith-grasp. This moment may not be

87. Knight, "Transformation of the Human Heart," 48.
88. Collins, *Holy Love*, 295.
89. Collins, "Topography of the Heart," 174.
90. "The Scripture Way of Salvation," *Works* VI: 53.
91. Collins, "Topography of the Heart," 174.

immediately perceptible to the emotions.[92] Awareness in entire sanctification may vary according to differences in circumstances and personality types. Furthermore, the expectation of a certain form for entire sanctification obscures its purely salvific character, a matter of the free, gracious act of God. Instantaneity is not a function of the form of religious experience, but rather, the nature of the experience as an instantiation of faith and grace, a work of the Holy Spirit through the merits of Jesus Christ.

Deliverance from Inbred Sin

Since the fundamental character of inherited sin is unbelief, entire sanctification must include the reversal of unbelief with faith, by the Holy Spirit. The faith continuum constitutes a progressive reversal of unbelief through the increase of faith. Entire sanctification marks the moment when this reversal is complete and the believer is full of faith, or, to use Wesley's term, faith is "unmixed." Since entire sanctification dispels the principle of unbelief, faith is not merely a condition for the experience, but is also an element of the purifying work of the Holy Spirit. The Holy Spirit expels unbelief by the impartation of faith. Deliverance from unbelief means that the believer trusts God wholeheartedly. The idea of salvation as a reversal of unbelief is consistent with the concept of faith as personal knowledge of God. This dynamic construal means that the life of faith subsequent to regeneration includes growing awareness of the principle of unbelief as well as increasing faith for deliverance. Entire sanctification is a logical step in the faith continuum of divine approach and human response. Deliverance from sin is not an end in itself, but rather, a restoration of the Divine Presence in fellowship, likeness and unity. "In this the steps away from God in alienation and depravity are matched by the steps back."[93] Entire sanctification is a significant reverse step from deprivation to restoration of fellowship, and from corruption to holiness.

The knowledge of God also reveals and cleanses away idolatry. Cleansing from idolatry is separation from other allegiances, one dimension of heart purity.[94] It is cleansing of the "residue of resistance to the

---

92. Taylor, *Theological Formulation*, 184. For example, Taylor describes the case of the believer who only realizes after the fact that he has been entirely sanctified. This realization came through observation of a change in his overall disposition.

93. Ibid., 107.

94. Ibid., 162.

Lordship of Christ."[95] Fullness of faith, or complete reliance upon God, delivers the believer from other allegiances. Acknowledgement of the sufficiency of the one Lord draws the believer into surrendering other allegiances as unnecessary and libelous to the character of God. Full affirmation of God's right to human trust and allegiance is the shift from partial to wholehearted love for God.

Deliverance from the principle of unbelief and idolatry constitutes freedom from the propensity to evil. Thus, entire sanctification may be understood as cleansing from the corruption of sin. The Holy Spirit cleanses the pervasive influence of sin upon all the believer's faculties, inclinations and dispositions. Entire sanctification "entails freedom from such unholy tempers as pride, self-will, and love of the world. . . . The believer now 'feels' no contrary principle within; the heart has been cleansed by the sanctifying presence of the Holy Spirit."[96] The single principle of being, knowing, and doing is holy love, producing a spirit of humility and patience.[97] Cleansing is not to be understood as the removal of a substance. Instead, it is a purification that effects undivided allegiance to God. Purification means the dissolution of unbelief and false allegiances, as well as their attendant moral corruption. Thus, cleansing may be understood as the annulment, abolition or destruction of the sin principle.[98] In sum, cleansing is not the removal of "something" but rather, the expulsion of the pervasive principle of unholiness by the revelation of God.

Deliverance from unbelief and idolatry is an instantiation of the faith-grace interaction. The cleansing work of the Holy Spirit is by faith. As the Holy Spirit imparts the knowledge of faith—the revelation of the divine nature of holy love, and of the corrupted human nature—the believer's posture is abject repentance that cries, "My Lord and my God," and "Woe is me." The precise moment of human acknowledgement of divine transcendence and condescension is a divine-human transaction that changes the quality of fellowship—it is both the divine impartation of faith, and the human exercise of faith.

---

95. Taylor, *Theological Formulation*, 163.

96. Collins, *Holy Love*, 302.

97. Ibid., 302.

98. Wiley, *Christian Theology*, 2: 490.

Divine Self-Giving

Purification of the heart is by the revelation of divine holiness and love. The work of the Holy Spirit in entire sanctification is that which He does by His very presence. The revelation of His holy love is sufficient for liberation from sin, enablement of the human partner for and establishment of fullness of communion. Divine self-giving is the fullness of the Holy Spirit's presence that expels sin and brings the believer under His lordship. Although the Holy Spirit abides with the believer from the moment of regeneration, in entire sanctification He assumes sovereignty. From this perspective, entire sanctification is neither for purity nor power; it is the out-pouring of God's own Spirit of holy love, whose abiding presence is purity and power.

The fullness of the Holy Spirit's presence actualizes divine sovereignty in the believer's life. In fellowship with God, allegiance to divine lordship is the only appropriate human stance. "Other sacrifices from us he would not, but the living sacrifice of the heart hath he chosen. Let it be continually offered up to God through Christ, in flames of holy love. And let no creature be suffered to share with him. *He will reign without a rival.*"[99] Entire sanctification is the beginning of the sovereign rule of God in the heart, and communion with Him free from unbelief and idolatry.

This is the purifying work of the Holy Spirit through His very presence. Taylor describes fullness of the Spirit as "completion, full of, wholly occupied with, completely under the influence of." To be filled with the Spirit is to be pervaded by His presence and to be completely under His influence.[100] This, in essence, is the relation of the Holy Spirit to the believer upon entire sanctification. In Eph 5:18 "be filled" means permeated, possessed, and dominated.[101] Thus, the term "fullness" with regards the Spirit's self-giving in entire sanctification means that the believer is "filled with all the fullness of God" (Eph 3:19). The purpose and the result of entire sanctification is the mutual "in-ness" of the believer and Christ through the Spirit. In other words, divine self-giving in entire sanctification refers to divine self-revelation—knowledge of God that brings the individual into entire participation in the divine fellowship of holy love.

99. "The Circumcision of the Heart," *Works* V: 211; "Plain Account," *Works* XI: 368 (italics mine).

100. Taylor, *Theological Formulation*, 188. This definition is based on the two words most commonly used in expressing Spirit-fullness in the New Testament.

101. Easley, "The Pauline Usage of Pneumati," 307.

The fullness of the Spirit does not negate the giving of the Holy Spirit in the new birth, but is to be distinguished from it. While the Holy Spirit comes to abide in the new believer, entire sanctification constitutes the beginning of His complete Lordship because even as He cleanses away inherited sin, He begins to exercise an influence which had formerly been obstructed by an antithetical principle. In this new kind of fellowship, He completes the work of making the believer holy. Furthermore, the idea of fullness must also be connected to the new human capacity for fellowship, which arises through liberation from inherited sin. He cleanses away inbred sin and frees the believer for fullness of communion in and through His self-outpouring. Thus, to speak of the second work of grace as the infilling with the Holy Spirit does not infer a type of piece-meal giving of the Spirit. Instead, the abiding Holy Spirit has been wooing the believer all along the way, in the faith continuum of genuine reciprocity, to this point in their fellowship where the believer's faith-grasp allows the Spirit full access and lordship over the human heart. It is the case that genuine reciprocity not only requires the believer's obedience, but it also requires full allegiance to Christ as Lord. Entire sanctification makes this quality of relation possible.

The initializing of the fullness of the Spirit may be considered under the metaphor of baptism, but does not necessarily correlate with the Pentecost event. As noted in chapter 2, in the nineteenth-century Holiness Movement entire sanctification came to be explicated in the Pentecost paradigm. This view as been called into question amongst Wesleyan scholars as it seems to find little support in Scripture.[102] Moreover, for

102. Turner, "The Baptism of the Holy Spirit," 61. Turner identifies two key questions regarding the correlation of entire sanctification with the pentecostal baptism with the Holy Spirit: "(1) Is the phrase "baptize in the Holy Spirit" descriptive of initiation into the Christian life, or is it a gift of the Spirit for cleansing and empowering for those who are already believers? (2) Is this expression, as commonly used in the Holiness Movement, a derivative from Wesleyan theology or is it a subsequent accretion that is without precedent either in Scripture or the usage of the Wesleys?" He succinctly states the argument against this correlation: "(1)The absence of a link between the work of the Holy Spirit and cleansing from sin in most standard works of theology, including those by many Wesleyan theologians. (2) Studies by Wesleyan scholars who have sought in vain for a clear teaching by Wesley that the baptism in the Holy Spirit is to be linked with entire sanctification. (3) The lack of an exhortation in the New Testament epistles that believers are to seek the baptism in the Holy Spirit. (4) Definitive exegetical studies which seek to demonstrate that the New Testament always associates the baptism in the Holy Spirit with the initiation into the Christian life. (5) Researchers who conclude that baptism in the Holy Spirit, as simultaneous with entire sanctification was a concept introduced into historical theology early in the nineteenth century and is neither scriptural nor Wesleyan."

Wesley, a justified person is a temple of the Holy Spirit.[103] Entire sanctification is the occasion in which the Holy Spirit gives Himself fully to the measure of human capacity. That capacity is necessarily greater through deliverance from inherited sin. Describing entire sanctification as the outpouring of Holy Spirit in His fullness means this experience marks a qualitative change in divine-human fellowship. Fullness refers to complete openness to and wholehearted love for God. But its principal characteristic is the unopposed exercise of the Holy Spirit's lordship—a relationship that only begins upon cleansing from inherited sin.

Viewing the work of the Holy Spirit as self-giving connects entire sanctification to the *ordo salutis* in two ways. First, it affirms the new birth because it is a full appropriation of the sanctifying grace which begins in the new birth. Second, it makes entire sanctification an outcome of the experiential knowledge of God which progressively arises in the *ordo salutis*. Nonetheless, it affirms a second instantaneous work of grace by showing that this experience is necessary for fellowship to reach its full qualitative potential.

Furthermore, from the standpoint of divine self-giving, the fullness of the Spirit is not for personal power and purity. The strong emphasis on the transformative and empowering effect of grace, as understood in Wesleyan soteriology, carries the attendant danger of understanding entire sanctification as the occasion of empowerment rather than as a quest for the Holy Spirit who graciously transforms and empowers the human partner by His presence and fellowship. The description of entire sanctification as "a cleansing away of Adamic depravity and an empowerment for witnessing and for the holy life" tends to detract from this truth.[104] Instead, from the communion perspective, entire sanctification is the free and gracious self-giving of the Holy Spirit, which liberates the human partner from sin and for full participation in divine holiness and love.

Human Self-Giving

Divine self-giving enables the believer to respond with full self-giving. The changed relationship with God includes separation from sin, devotement to God, full self-giving, and mutual indwelling:

103. Journal Entry, October 29, 1762, *Works* VII: 120
104. Grider, *A Wesleyan-Holiness Theology*, 367.

> The work of sanctification involves not only a separation from sin, but a separation to God. This positive devotement, however, is something more than the human consecration of the soul to God. It represents, also, the Holy Spirit's acceptance of the offering, and, therefore, a divine empowering or enduement. It is a divine possession, and the spring and energy of this spiritual devotement is holy love. The Spirit of God, as the spirit of perfect consecration is able as the Sanctifier, not only to fill the soul with love, but to awaken love in return.[105]

Wiley's explication illuminates the remarkable intimacy that arises between the Spirit and the believer in entire sanctification. It marks out several facets of union with Christ. First, deliverance from sin is clearly not an end in itself. It is not for the believer's holiness. Instead, abandonment of false allegiances and unbelief is in tandem with divine revelation of holy love to the believer's heart. The response is thus full self-giving. Further, the Spirit's self-giving is an outpouring of holy love, an actualization of God's demonstration of love in Jesus Christ. Although, for the purpose of clear explanation, we have considered the discrete elements of entire sanctification—repentance, faith, deliverance from sin, divine self-giving and human self-giving—in separate sections, these are all aspects of the single experience of God's mysterious interaction with the believer. Entire sanctification is a transformative moment, not only because of the resulting moral transformation, but because this experience is a unique, revelatory, and salvific encounter with God that is at a level of intimacy and depth that the believer had not previously experienced.

Freedom from unbelief is freedom for God. In entire sanctification, the Holy Spirit turns the believer away from the tendency to seek other loves, or to depart from the living God as the source of life and meaning. Freedom from the principle of unbelief is essentially freedom for God, or in Wesley's terms, an enlargement of the spiritual senses, or fullness of faith. The believer now has the capacity to trust God entirely. Wholehearted faith implies an enlarged capacity for fellowship with God, "complete openness to the Heavenly Father."[106] The effect of this openness is a deep sense of intimacy and belonging, and a heart transformed by holy love.

Enlarged capacity for God means that the human partner is also able to give the self freely to God. As mentioned earlier, one aspect of consecration is repentance from idolatry. Consecration also means

105. Wiley, *Christian Theology*, 2: 491.
106. Dunning, *Grace, Faith and Holiness*, 488.

wholehearted self-giving, not as a *condition* of entire sanctification, but as a grace-enabled movement towards God that is an element of the new relationship established in entire sanctification. As St. Paul urges, "by the mercies of God, present your bodies as living sacrifices, holy and acceptable to God, which is your spiritual service of worship (Rom 12:1 NASB)." A. T. Robertson makes several notable comments regarding human self-giving in relation to this text. First, he states that it is "by means of" divine mercy that the believer can make this sacrifice. Second, the use of the first aorist active imperative (*paristimi*) suggests that self-giving must be an immediate and completed action. Third, the reference to "a living sacrifice" is in contrast to a slain sacrifice, such that the command entails awareness of and capacity to make this sacrifice.[107] The thrust of these insights is that human self-giving in entire sanctification is a worshipful and rational response to the revelation of Jesus the Lord directly to the believer's heart, through the Holy Spirit. Furthermore, as Rob Staples observes, fullness of communion requires that the human partner reciprocates through faith-grasp and self-giving.[108] God's enablement of the human partner to respond in free self-giving discloses another dimension of grace.

The ability to surrender to God freely and entirely is not possible except through the freeing and enabling prior work of the Holy Spirit in cleansing. The cleansing, self-giving action of the Spirit precedes the human response of allegiance, self-giving and receptivity. Sacrificial love belongs to God, and only as He imparts love can the believer respond. This construal asserts that all salvation is only by faith, and that the action of God is always prior. In essence, complete self-giving in the experience of entire sanctification is a genuine, worshipful acknowledgement of divine sovereignty, expressed to the fullest extent by complete self-giving.

Fullness of Communion and Holiness

This third section addresses the transformative impact of the new divine-human relation established in entire sanctification. Holiness is not the product of entire sanctification alone. Instead, holiness comes through participation in God. Yet, entire sanctification liberates the believer from all that stands against the Spirit of holy love. As such, it purifies the heart.

107. Robertson, "Word Pictures of the New Testament."
108. Staples, "John Wesley's Doctrine of the Holy Spirit," 93–94.

Without the impediment of inbred sin, and in the new intimacy that comes in entire sanctification, the believer increasingly bears the fruit of holiness.

Participation and Holiness

Human holiness comes through participation in God. Holiness is "sharing in the divine Trinitarian life, in as far as is possible for a mere human."[109] The indwelling Holy Spirit is the cause of holiness.[110] The revelation of God in the salvific missions of the Son and the Spirit has in view the restoration of the human partner to holiness and happiness. Divine self-disclosure points to this gracious purpose. Revelation is an expression of God's freedom to be *for* and *with* the creature. "That this 'giving' happens in his beloved Son is assurance that God's sovereign holiness is that which stoops down to us in merciful condescension and at great cost."[111] Holiness theology affirms the extraordinary truth that "holiness tabernacles among us in Jesus Christ. At Pentecost holiness was extended to all who call upon this Name, as God creates for Himself a holy nation, a people for his own possession (1 Pet 2:9)."[112] The work of entire sanctification actualizes this divine purpose by destroying sin in the believer through the fullness of the Spirit's indwelling. Moreover, fullness of communion ushers in a deeper participation in God, which includes the Spirit's Lordship. As Lord, He influences the believer's motivations, attitudes and dispositions.

It may be argued that orientation to fellowship rather than to the ethical imperative produces a holiness theology that is vulnerable to antinomianism. However, Wesley, who constantly sought to avoid this very danger and insisted upon the need for *living* holiness, avoids legalism and moralism, as well as antinomianism, by the affirmation that because God works, believers can and must work.[113] The believer can only thrive in fellowship with God through right moral choices. As such, believers must put on Christ and live in accordance with divine lordship. This approach grounds the possibility and necessity of holy living in the constant availability of empowering grace through

109. Dorr, "Nature of Holiness," 237.

110. "A Letter to a Roman Catholic," *Works* X: 82.

111. Goroncy, "Recovered Holiness,"200.

112. Ibid., 199.

113. "On Working out Our Own Salvation," *Works* VI: 511.

the indwelling Holy Spirit. A heart completely set on God means a life lived for the sake of God. This is the root of holiness—we become what we know. Thus, the quest for God for His own sake underwrites the imperative of living a holy life. As knowledge increases by faith, the believer grows up in the likeness of Christ through obedience.

Transformation or sanctification begins at the new birth and continues throughout life in both the continuous divine-human fellowship as well as the decisive moments of regeneration and entire sanctification. In the decisive moment of entire sanctification, the Holy Spirit cleanses the believer from inherited sin through His full self-giving. Subsequent to this experience, the Holy Spirit's control enables the believer to thrive in holiness, without the obstruction of sin and through the new fullness of the Spirit's indwelling. Fellowship with God "produces both good works and holiness."[114] Moreover, "faith forms love."[115] In sum, the salvific continuum restores the knowledge of God, which is the source of human holiness.

Transformation through Crisis and Process

The instantaneous transformation in entire sanctification constitutes a change in heart allegiance. The transformative effect of this new relation is that holy love is the moral power of the believer's life. Holy love determines the disposition and desires of the believer. The deep-seated intentionality of human existence, that which conditions the quality of relationships, is holy love. Yet, this transformation of motivation and determination is to be worked out in the daily exigencies of life.

The effect of the crisis transformation increasingly shapes the believer's existential reality as the believer lives in submission to divine lordship. Taylor observes that the indwelling Spirit alters our value systems, shows us what is important, and makes us aware of the chaotic areas of life. This ensures that all aspects of existence progressively harmonize with holy love. The Holy Spirit's Lordship extends to every facet of life. Fellowship with Him thrives as the believer obediently corrects thoughts, attitudes and choices as He sheds light.[116] In sum, "The subsequent life of holiness is ethical inasmuch as it requires ever-new choices and re-affirmations of the basic commitment to God and right. But this daily

114. Williams, *Wesley's Theology Today*, 107.

115. Ibid., 107.

116. Taylor, *Theological Formulation*, 193.

commitment is no longer a daily struggle against the deepest grain of our nature, but a natural bent, made natural by grace, so that our service of obedience can be rendered in freedom and with joy."[117] On this view, the crisis experience of entire sanctification establishes a new relation which finds increasingly greater expression through its daily actualization in all aspects of human existence.

Consideration of transformation as both crisis and process alleviates concerns about the over-valuation of the crisis experience. In entire sanctification, grace transforms human intentionality. The life of fullness of communion advances through choices that reflect the new intentionality. While the power of changed intentionality is not to be understated, the life of holiness as an ongoing fellowship points to a progressive transformation which entails discipline and obedience.

Inward and Outward Transformation

As the believer outwardly manifests the inward change, outward manifestation nourishes the inward change. Fellowship with God can only thrive as it translates into love for the other.

In "On Zeal" Wesley describes the inter-relation of inward and outward holiness flowing from fellowship with God. He states,

> In a Christian believer love sits upon the throne which is erected in the inmost soul: namely, love of God and man, and which fills the whole heart, and reigns without a rival. In a circle near the throne are all holy tempers; – longsuffering, gentleness, meekness, fidelity, temperance; and if any other were comprised in "the mind which was in Christ Jesus." In an exterior circle are all the works of mercy, whether to the souls or bodies of men. By these we exercise all holy tempers; by means of grace, although this is not commonly adverted to. Next to these are those that are usually termed works of piety; – reading and hearing the word, public, family, private prayer, receiving the Lord's Supper, fasting or abstinence. Lastly, that his followers may the more effectively provoke one another to love, holy tempers, and good works, our Lord has united them together in one body, the Church a little emblem of which we have in every particular Christian congregation.[118]

117. Taylor, *Theological Formulation*, 43.
118. "On Zeal," *Works* VII: 60–61.

Inward transformation begins with the purification of the heart with holy love and flows into the dispositions that characterize human relationships. The foregoing excerpt from Wesley suggests the following four steps in the expression of love through attitudes and choices.

First, the primary transformation is the reign of love in the believer's heart through the Holy Spirit, that is, the controlling presence of the Holy Spirit. However, the love of God cannot be abstracted from the holiness of God, nor can holiness and love be conflated into a single principle. Instead, "in philosophical terms of personality, holiness represents self-grasp, and love the self-communication; hence holiness logically precedes and must be regarded as the peculiar quality of that nature out of which love flows."[119] The implication for human transformation is that holiness is the quality of the love which becomes one's controlling principle in entire sanctification. Thus, holiness imparts ethical character to the believer's love. The inward reign of holy love then, means that love is not mere sentiment, or kindly feelings. Instead, it is the righteousness of God, which, by faith, has come to indwell the believer, and qualitatively conditions love and its expression.

Second, the controlling principle of holy love progressively transforms the believer's frame of mind. The Wesleyan terms, "disposition" and "temper" are inherent and durable qualities of the heart.[120] Holy tempers refer to holiness of character or mind-set, described as "longsuffering, gentleness, meekness" and the like. These attitudes indicate the outward orientation of one's mind towards the other. Wesley's understanding of holy tempers corresponds with the fruit of the Holy Spirit (Gal 5:22–23). The first step in transformation is the alignment of one's frame of mind with the holy love of God. The transference of love to the level of one's attitudes and disposition requires disciplined and sustained pursuit of godliness.

Third, works of mercy express a holy frame of mind. For Wesley, being good means doing good. Inward transformation becomes visible as the outwardly-oriented mind looks to the other and *sees* the need of the other. Awareness of the needs of others is only possible by this outward focus. One responds to the needs of others by the works of mercy—actions that contribute to the overall well-being of persons. Doing works of mercy helps the believer to develop greater sensitivity to the needs of others. The works of mercy are responses to the needs of others. In responding, one develops

---

119. Wiley, *Christian Theology*, 2: 492.
120. Collins, "Topography of the Heart," 165.

more sensitivity and kind-heartedness. Therefore, inward transformation is both nurtured by and expressed in works of mercy.

Fourth, works of piety foster fellowship with God and neighbor. The works of piety, such as prayer, Bible study, the fellowship of believers, ensure that outward expression continues to find its source in the inward life with God. Failure to keep the Wesleyan balance at this point leads to over-emphasis on either inwardness or outwardness. Undue emphasis on inward transformation is the path to a mystical religion that is blind to the clear biblical teaching of practical love for one's neighbor. On the other hand, over-emphasis on outwardness dissociates works of mercy from their source in the holy love of God, resulting in actions that are not always motivated by love. The interconnection of works of mercy and works of piety shows the need for balance between inwardness and outwardness in the life of faith.

Wesley's vision is of a life in God by faith through grace as the center and source of human transformation. Inward and outward transformation are indissolubly linked, since the former finds expression in the latter, and the latter nurtures the former. Fellowship with God grows as faith works through love. Thus, human transformation is both crisis and process, inward and outward. Inward transformation becomes gradually evident as the believer's interactions take on the virtues of love, peace, joy, patience, goodness, self control, and the like. These increasingly restore wholeness to individuals and relationships in the context of the fellowship of believers.

Conclusion

This chapter has shown that in entire sanctification, divine-human fellowship reaches a decisive moment of faith in which the Holy Spirit cleanses away inherited sin and draws the believer into fullness of communion. The *ordo salutis* is a divine-human fellowship of increasing knowledge of God by faith. Entire sanctification arises within this framework. The definition of sin as a pervasive principle of idolatry and unbelief highlights its character as antithetical to the knowledge of God and the lordship of Jesus Christ. In a complete reversal of unbelief, the Holy Spirit gives the believer wholehearted faith and the capacity to renounce false allegiances. The Holy Spirit assumes control of the believer's heart, and holy love becomes the pervasive principle of human existence. In one sense, deliverance from inbred sin completes the inward transformation or sanctification which began in the new birth, because sin no longer impedes love. In another sense, inward transformation becomes more consistent and fruitful under the controlling influence of the Holy Spirit and finds expression in love for the other.

The treatment of entire sanctification in this chapter illuminates the *ordo salutis* of genuine reciprocity as the necessary locus of entire sanctification. Moreover, it affirms the salvific character of the experience by stressing that it is by faith alone. The *ordo salutis* itself, and entire sanctification within it, is rooted in divine grace as the cause and source of human holiness. Grace is the cause of divine overture and human response. It destroys the pervasive principle of sin that stands in the way of divine-human fellowship. Grace arises out of the holy love of God, as an expression of His free purpose to draw human partners into fellowship with Himself. Entire sanctification, as explained in this chapter, ultimately refers theological reflection to the triune fellowship because the experience is for full participation therein. As such, this account of entire sanctification is theocentric and experiential rather than self-referential.

5

Fullness of Communion

The Ecclesial Significance of Entire Sanctification

Introduction

PRECEDING CHAPTERS HAVE DEMONSTRATED that experiential knowledge of God by faith includes entire sanctification, an experience that commences fullness of communion. The communion perspective explicitly relates entire sanctification to the triune fellowship and salvific mission. As such, the communion model illuminates grace as the basis of genuine reciprocity. The pursuit of fullness of communion is a worthwhile ecclesial purpose. When, through the means of grace, ecclesial life intentionally orients to fullness of communion the church develops doxological corporate character, distinctive identity within the Christian tradition, and passion for the divine mission. The single-minded quest for fellowship with God, over time, produces doxological ecclesial culture, since to know God is to love and worship Him. Thus, the church is the community in which salvation by faith translates into doxology by faith. The church pursues this transcendent purpose through consistent use of the means of grace, in continual surrender to the Spirit's Lordship, and in expectation of deepening intimacy with God and one another. In this locus of intentionality, the church lives in hopeful perseverance and joyful expectation of fullness of communion through entire sanctification. The resulting ecclesial culture is not only doxological, but also inclusive, since all members of the community engage in the same quest through the same means. A Christian community oriented to fullness of communion derives its missional rationale from its passion for the divine mission, since participation in God includes participation in His vision and His mission. Through engagement with God's passion, the church becomes a means of grace.

Doxological Corporate Identity

The motif of communion is simultaneously salvific and doxological. The fundamental precept of Wesleyan soteriology is that salvation is partici-patory knowledge of God by faith. Salvation culminates in doxological *habitus* since to know God is to love Him and become like Him. Com-mon, intentional pursuit of the knowledge of God shapes the church in doxological character. The Holy Spirit actualizes divine condescension as He gives Himself to the church in fellowship. This is a reality of grace that belongs to the church by virtue of the Christological promise, "I am with you to the end of the age" (Matt 28:20), ratified by the pentecostal divine self-outpouring. On this basis, the church can confidently expect the presence of the Holy Spirit as its distinctive privilege. The church universal can seek the knowledge of God and invite others to join this quest. Thus, although undertaken through diverse forms, the quest for the knowledge of God transcends traditions. This shared quest provides a basis for ecumenical fellowship.

Doxological Character

The pursuit of the knowledge of God shapes the church in doxological character, since the church seeks the knowledge of God in the attitudes of worship—submission, adoration, and allegiance. Over time, the attitudes of worship become the ecclesial *habitus*.

Submission is the acknowledgement that the presence and action of the Holy Spirit is the fountain-head of the church's existence. He shapes the church's self-understanding as an entity called forth and sustained in being through His presence. The church submits to the Spirit's admin-istration of redemption in ecclesial life by acknowledging that it lives by the Holy Spirit, that all its help must come and actually comes from God alone, and that it has no innate redemptive possibility apart from the divine life. This is the requisite disposition for fellowship with God because it sets the right relation between the church and its Lord (Eph

5:24). Seeking fellowship with God in a submissive attitude is worship because it is the acknowledgement of being the purchased possession of the one Lord. Moreover, to know God is to worship Him as Lord. Thus, submission is the stance in which the church seeks the knowledge of God and it is also the attitude shaped by the knowledge of God.

The primary act of corporate submission is the prayer, "Thy will be done" (Matt 6:10), through which the church seeks grace for submission and enacts submission through prayer. The church asks for enablement to submit to the divine will because it believes that the divine will must be actualized in the church by the Holy Spirit. When the church prays for the manifestation of the divine will, the prayer itself is an act of submission to the divine will. In sum, the prayer, "Thy will be done" is an act of submission because the church acts in submission by so praying; and the content of the prayer is itself a supplication for God to impart a spirit of submission to the church. Included in the prayer of submission is supplication for fullness of communion through entire sanctification, since, by this experience, the church may know God in deeper fellowship and fully surrender to His lordship.

The church enacts submission through corporate obedience to the divine will in a life of holiness. This obedience is an act of submission because it is a positive expression of the church's dependence on grace. For Wesley, a welcoming attitude to the Holy Spirit means that the church must not sin. Sins do not reflect submission "because they are so many contempts of the highest expression of his love. . . . Every sin we now commit is done in despite of all his powerful assistances, in defiance of his reproofs."[1] The church expresses its desire for fellowship with God by living in accordance with His nature of holy love, and demonstrates enabling grace by its capacity for holy living.

As the church perseveres in the stance of submission, it knows that it is the Spirit who shapes the attitude of submission and that He actualizes His lordship in ecclesial life. Submission is therefore an exercise of faith, and a worshipful posture in which the church experiences deepening communion with God. As such, submission draws the church into fullness of communion. The Holy Spirit shapes the church in submission by the revelation of His lordship since it is in this attitude that the church seeks the knowledge of God and knows God.

1. "Grieving the Holy Spirit," *Works*, VII: 487.

God reveals Himself as the holy, transcendent Lord. His self-disclosure of transcendent holiness is also the disclosure of merciful condescension, for self-disclosure is condescension, which is revealed as such by divine transcendence. The knowledge that it is the transcendent God who thus condescends in free grace—in Jesus Christ, and through the Holy Spirit's presence and action in the church—is adoration. Thus, "adoration is an acknowledgement of God's transcendence made possible by the fact that he is also self-giving."[2] The church takes the stance of adoration as the Spirit imparts the realization of His present-ness, which moves heart and mind to the cross and towards the holy God who condescends. Thus, under the revealing work of the Spirit the church knows and worships the triune God. The knowledge of God arises increasingly as believers experience deepening fellowship with God. In this fellowship, the Holy Spirit reveals the divine nature of holy love and draws the church into the divine perichoretic fellowship. The revelation of holy love elicits adoration of the Holy Trinity. Adoration of the Trinity shapes ecclesial fellowship and draws the church towards fullness of communion. Therefore, the quest for the knowledge of God shapes worshipful corporate character which itself draws the church forward in this quest.

The church adores the Holy Trinity through self-giving. Wainwright suggests that the self-giving of Jesus presents a paradigm for worship. The self-emptying of Jesus "stands at the heart of the communion between humanity and God; it may even correspond, within the sphere of time, to the eternal perichoresis by which . . . the divine Persons empty themselves into each other and receive each other's fullness."[3] The Holy Spirit reveals the worshipful character of the Son's self-giving, and directs the gaze of the church to the divine nature of sacrificial love. This revelation draws the church into the response of self-giving, a human reflection of the divine life. Wainwright observes, "True worship implies self-giving love on the part of the worshippers who are thus responsively reflecting the self-giving love which God displayed towards humanity in the gift of Jesus Christ and which Christ himself displayed in his relations both with the 'the Father' and with his fellow human beings."[4] The church's self-outpouring is an expression of adoration. Adoration of the Trinity informs ecclesial fellowship because it allows God to shape the church into the image of the divine

2. Wainwright, *Doxology*, 37.

3. Ibid., 23.

4. Ibid., 107.

fellowship.[5] Thus, holy love, made visible in the self-outpouring of the transcendent God, shapes the church into a self-giving fellowship.

Mutual self-giving, which describes the divine approach and the church's adoring response, draws the church towards fullness of communion. As the church makes fellowship with God its primary concern, the Holy Spirit imparts grace for this fellowship. As fellowship deepens, the church experiences fullness of communion through entire sanctification. Deepening fellowship with God is itself adoration of the Holy Trinity. Salvation by faith resolves into doxology as the church orients to communion with God.

Submission and adoration evoke allegiance to God, which the church demonstrates by committing ecclesial resources to the quest for fellowship with God. Therefore, "the church must pattern its life after the communion of the Trinity, providing structures, relationships, and practices for instruction and nurture in the faith."[6] The use of resources in ways that reflect sacrificial love and that are conducive to the quest for the knowledge of God expresses allegiance to God. Moreover, the church shows allegiance to God by refusing to establish an idolatrous relationship to its structures, programs and funds. Fundamentally, allegiance to God in ecclesial life requires complete reliance upon God as the source of its help, and commitment of its resources to the divine mission.

To conclude, submission, adoration, and allegiance are doxological attitudes in which the church seeks the knowledge of God, and which are shaped by the knowledge of God. The quest for the knowledge of God results in these attitudes becoming a corporate *habitus*. The orientation to fullness of communion draws the church into a single soteriological-doxological focus, which gives ecclesial life a worthwhile transcendent purpose.

Worship as Divine-Human Encounter

In the doxological matrix of submission, adoration and allegiance, the church lives in the expectation and experience of fullness of communion and approaches public corporate worship as an event of personal encounter with God. Worship is the sanctifying experience of encounter with God through the liturgy. Thus, in public worship, believers draw into closer fellowship with God.

5. Meeks, "Trinity, Community, and Power," 24.
6. Matthaei, "Transcripts of the Trinity," 128–29.

Corporate worship is the celebration of God, a mutual gift of enjoyment. It is personal encounter with God. "In worship we encounter the God revealed in Jesus Christ, who is present by way of the Holy Spirit, and made known to us through faith, which is a gift of the Holy Spirit."[7] The church recognizes and responds to divine self-disclosure as the Holy Spirit actualizes divine power, love and holiness in the midst of believers. Worship affirms and expresses the personal relation between God and His people: "The character of Christian worship is that of an encounter in which God speaks to us and gives us the tokens of his love, and in which we offer him our praise and thanks, seek his forgiveness and renew our commitment, ask his help and entrust our future to him. Our knowledge of God is therefore 'personal knowledge.'"[8] In worship, the church acknowledges the need for divine grace, and expresses gratitude for the reality of grace that comes through Jesus and is actualized by the Holy Spirit. It acknowledges God's faithfulness in imparting grace through the attitudes of submission, adoration and allegiance. Since, in order to sustain its existence, the church repeatedly asks for and receives grace, it attests to divine faithfulness by every new worship event in which it asks anew for forgiveness and help. When the church worships God it knows that God is present and enables worship. Thus, corporate worship is the space "where God and human beings each give and receive in an exchange which is their mutual communion."[9]

The elements of worship mediate divine-human encounter through the Holy Spirit. "The object of our knowing, God, is mediated by the elements of worship. But there is a surplus of meaning that exceeds the sum of the parts much as a physiognomy exceeds each of the individual features."[10] Thus, although divine-human encounter is mediated by the elements of worship, the experience transcends the material means. The elements of worship facilitate the remembrance of God or *anamnesis*, and this repeated recollection acts transformatively in the lives of worshippers.[11]

Liturgy and hymnody draw heart and mind into hearing God. Liturgy is "the place where an ecclesial group preserves its traditions, symbols,

---

7. Knight, "Worship and Sanctification," 14.

8. Wainwright, *Doxology*, 443.

9. Ibid., 20.

10. Wood, "The Liturgy," 111.

11. Ibid., 109.

and texts and expresses its self-identity."[12] Liturgy creates a historical and temporal space for participatory knowledge of God.[13] Hymns are avenues to express amazement at God's grace, amazement which transcends reason, and reaches, in Wainwright's terms, "ecstatic reason"—where prose gives way to poetry, where the innermost wellsprings of gratitude and praise transcend words.[14] The church expects God to come through elements of worship, "from the transcendence of heaven," to enter "into the very marrow of our being."[15] The church expects this encounter with God because it has already experienced the transcendent God of grace through these means.

In this space of worship, and within the ecclesial ethos of doxology, the Holy Spirit sanctifies believers and draws them into fullness of communion. Knight demonstrates the essential link between worship and sanctification. "It is as we praise and thank God that, through remembering again and again who God is and what God has done, we grow in the knowledge and love of God."[16] As such, worship does not merely provide "information about God which we cognitively appropriate and then will to emulate."[17] Instead, authentic worship is remembering what God has done and who He is, as revealed in Scripture. Remembering is more than a cognitive act. It is a deep awareness in the heart and mind of the reality of God. Through remembering, the gathered community "encounters the living reality of that God through the Spirit"[18] and is fashioned in holiness and love through this encounter. Appropriate response to God and desire for God become possible as the church reflects on the Incarnation, Crucifixion, Resurrection, and Pentecost, and as the Holy Spirit presents these reflections to the hearts of believers as salvific realities.

The experience of remembering in and with personal encounter glorifies God. As the church glorifies God, it is sanctified. Worship "is both for the glorification of God and the sanctification of persons, but it can only aid the latter if its focus is on the former."[19] Worship is remem-

---

12. Ibid., 100.

13. Ibid., 95.

14. Wainwright, *Doxology*, 200.

15. Ibid., 41.

16. Knight, "Worship and Sanctification," 14.

17. Ibid.

18. Ibid.

19. Ibid., 12.

bering "the God of Israel and of Jesus Christ as the ground and motive for its thanksgiving and praise."[20] As such, worship evokes "a response of love, hope, humility, joy, peace and gratitude."[21] This response is itself the sanctifying work of the Spirit in the hearts of worshippers. On this view sanctification is the return of love in response to the revelation of divine love through the worship encounter of God and His adoring church.

As the church remembers and glorifies God, it can expect the Holy Spirit to do His work of entire sanctification. The doxological stance signifies openness to the Holy Spirit, and He accomplishes the divine purpose of drawing believers into deeper communion. It follows that believers may experience this work of grace in a particular worship event. While public worship is not the only context for entire sanctification, it is a significant one since worship is a sanctifying encounter with God.

Catholicity and Distinctiveness

The quest for the knowledge of God is the privilege of the church universal as the Lukan account of the primitive church attests. Although various traditions may approach this quest in diverse ways, the quest itself transcends traditions. The ecclesial quest for the knowledge of God provides a basis for dialogue with other traditions and imparts distinctive character to the Wesleyan-Holiness tradition itself.

The primitive church as described in the Acts of the Apostles gives evidence of doxological corporate character, and orientation to fellowship as the lived experience of salvation by faith. At the outset, the disciples wait for the coming of the Holy Spirit before engaging in mission (2:1–14). Peter's address to the gathered crowd affirms that his act of proclamation is based on the divine promise of the Holy Spirit (2:17). In sum, the Lukan account portrays the utter dependence of the church upon the dynamic activity of the Holy Spirit.[22] The church demonstrates an attitude of praise in their fellowship (2:47) and in the midst of persecution. (4:23–24). The church's primary concern is to glorify God and accomplish of His will (4:27–30). Allegiance to God also characterizes the life of the primitive church. Peter and John attest to this allegiance before the Sanhedrin (4:19). Their aim is to accomplish the divine purpose regardless of personal cost.

20. Ibid., 14.

21. Ibid.

22. Deasley, "The Church in the Acts of the Apostles," 79.

These acts demonstrate a radical transfer of allegiance from prior loyalties to Jesus Christ alone. The locus of these expressions of submission, adoration and allegiance is their fellowship in the Holy Spirit.

The doxological stance of the primitive church suggests that the ecclesial ethos that arises from the communion paradigm is to be desired by the church catholic. In the Wesleyan-Holiness tradition, holiness theology in the communion paradigm provides a theological rational for orienting ecclesial life to the transcendent goal of worship and fellowship. Other traditions may obtain this orientation on other theological bases. There is potential for mutual enrichment as various traditions share their unique perspectives on the common quest for the knowledge of God. Moreover, not only can the Wesleyan-Holiness tradition identify with others on this basis, but it can also share its theological grounds for its quest for the knowledge of God. Undoubtedly, holiness theology can thus be perceived not merely as the particularity of one tradition, but as this tradition's singular contribution to the quest for the knowledge of God shared by the church catholic.

Within the Wesleyan-Holiness tradition, the communion paradigm allows holiness theology to be the underwriting theological principle of ecclesial life. Through the common quest for the knowledge of God, believers experience God in transformative ways. As such, focus on the knowledge of God brings believers into the experience of entire sanctification. Moreover, this orientation frees ecclesial life from a culture of self-involvement, and for participation in God and His mission. It brings to the church a genuine experience of love for the other, since, freed from subjectivism, the church can be aware of the other, which is a movement motivated by the imperative of love. Orientation to fullness of communion fosters inclusiveness in ecclesial life, since all members of the Christian community pursue the same goal through the same means. The single, common orientation is conducive to an open, inclusive culture. In addition, the attitudes of submission, allegiance and adoration draw attention to God and allow genuine spirituality to thrive in the locus of fellowship, which ultimately evokes deepening love. Thus, fullness of communion, through entire sanctification functions as a theological principle that sets the agenda for worship, fellowship and mission.

Summation

Holiness theology in the communion paradigm has the potential to shape a distinctive ecclesial identity. Orientation to fullness of communion produces a worshipful *habitus*. The church encounters God in corporate worship through which God reveals Himself and sanctifies His people. In addition, the communion perspective provides a basis for ecumenical fellowship. Proclamation of the holiness message in terms of communion introduces a spirit of inclusiveness in Christian fellowship. The result is that the Holy Spirit shapes the church into a redeemed and redemptive fellowship—a means of grace.

The Means of Grace

The means of grace are the creaturely elements of ecclesial life through which the Holy Spirit draws the church into the fellowship of holy love. Consistent and disciplined use of the means of grace produces doxological ecclesial culture. The means of grace equip the church to be the Body through which God calls others into fellowship with Himself. This section shows that believers thrive in the life of faith and experience entire sanctification through the means of grace, which appeal to both affective and cognitive faculties of knowing. As communal activities, the means of grace engage believers in the common quest for God in ways that honor individuality and promote accountability

The Knowledge of God through the Means of Grace

The means of grace are ecclesial activities through which the Holy Spirit imparts faith, and the church expresses faith through love. Thus, fellowship with God deepens through consistent use of the means of grace. Wesley distinguishes between the ordained and prudential means of grace.[23] Ordained means—Scripture, prayer, and the sacraments—are

---

23. Knight, *The Presence of God in the Christian Life*, 5. Knight identifies three categories of means of grace in the Wesley corpus: General means (universal obedience, keeping all the commandments, watching, denying ourselves, taking up our cross daily, exercise of the presence of God); instituted means (prayer, searching the Scripture, the Lord's supper, fasting, Christian conference); prudential means (particular rules of holy living, class and band meetings, prayer meetings, visiting the sick, doing all the good one can, doing no harm, reading edifying literature). The two categories treated

divinely required, while prudential means complement the ordained means in providing a wide range of avenues through which the church can grow in the knowledge of God.

The ordained means of grace are the divinely appointed channels of grace through which the Holy Spirit imparts grace.[24] Based on this definition, public worship, as described earlier, is a means of grace. Preaching is the central element of Christian worship and the principal means of grace. Preaching is proclamation of Jesus Christ as revealed in Scripture. The content, focus and aim of this proclamation is the revelation of Jesus Christ in the church. When Scripture is declared from this standpoint, preaching becomes revelation under the presence and power of the Holy Spirit.

The holy sacraments, baptism and the Eucharist, are ways to publicly remember and declare the Name of Jesus Christ. They are powerful symbols through which the Holy Spirit conveys grace. Baptism is participation in the death and resurrection of Jesus Christ (Rom 6:3–4). The event is sacramental because it draws the believer into union with Christ by faith, not by the material elements, but through them. Likewise, the creaturely elements of the Eucharist bring the power of atoning grace into the fellowship of believers, and the fellowship of believers into deeper fellowship with Christ and one another. The sacraments are means of grace because as the church seeks the knowledge of God through these means, the Holy Spirit uses these events in revelatory and salvific ways.

Prayer is a divine imperative and the principal means of the church's partnership with God for the manifestation of the divine will on earth. Prayer is asking for the divine will in all spheres of existence, as this will is revealed in Scripture. The church asks in obedience to the divine imperative. The church asks because divine integrity, wisdom and power guarantee the answer. Prayer is the means by which the Spirit directs the church's gaze to the right hand of the Majesty on high where the Son sits to intercede, to hear and answer prayer. Thus, even the church's most anguished outpouring is never desperate, because prayer frees the church from distress by drawing it into remembrance of its faithful Lord.

The prudential means of grace are activities, other than the ordained means of grace, that foster growth in faith. These include the works of piety and the works of mercy. The works of mercy are acts of love that express faith. Through the works of mercy, the believer exercises holy tempers and

in this book, ordained and prudential, cover the principal avenues of grace in ecclesial life. Those not treated primarily belong to the area of personal spiritual discipline.

24. "The Means of Grace," *Works* V: 187.

dispositions such as longsuffering, meekness, fidelity and temperance. The works of piety are activities that nurture spiritual growth.[25] Both works of mercy and works of piety nurture and express holy tempers, and holy tempers arise from a heart in which love reigns supreme.

The total effect of consistent use of the means of grace is to draw believers towards fullness of communion, and maturity in that fullness. First, unbelievers are brought to saving knowledge of Jesus Christ. Second, believers can use both ordained and prudential means of grace to grow in the knowledge of the Lord Jesus Christ. This growth brings awareness of inherited sin, so that believers can pray for entire sanctification. Subsequent to entire sanctification, believers continue to exercise faith through the means of grace and grow up in the fellowship of wholehearted love. As Wesley attests, "All who desire the grace of God are to wait for it in the means he hath ordained."[26] Although it is the Holy Spirit who entirely sanctifies, believers must wait for the experience by using the means of grace.

The community of believers thrives in fellowship with God by consistent use of the means of grace. "The role of community has to do with how the church participates in this process of growing in faith. Thus, the structures of the institutional church must be congruent with God's saving purposes."[27] Congregational life needs to be built up around the means of grace. This entails not only making the means of grace accessible, but also developing objectives in harmony with the transcendent ecclesial goal. In sum, the goal of particular ministries is to provide opportunities for fellowship with God and with one another. Furthermore, the means of grace must be offered in contextual form. Miles suggests that "Wesley's flexible and pragmatic approach to the prudential means of grace can give church leaders a model for making a similar list of means that could be fruitful for Christians today."[28] Contemporary forms of the prudential means of grace can include different kinds of praying, meditation and sacrificial giving.

The means of grace shape a cognitive schema which makes direct experience of God feasible and comprehensible. The knowledge of God, thus far stressed as personal and participatory, includes cognitive knowledge. Abraham remarks that the "knowledge of God is progressive,

---

25. "On Zeal," *Works* VII: 60 (Wesley's description of the works of piety includes the ordained means of grace—Scripture, prayer and receiving the Lord's Supper—as well as fasting, this latter to be considered a prudential means of grace).

26. "The Means of Grace," *Works* V: 198.

27. Matthaei, "Transcripts of the Trinity," 124.

28. Miles, "'The Arts of Holy Living,'" 151.

complex, multilayered, and informal. It is not merely a matter of propositional evidence, yet evidence and argument have a place. It is not merely a matter of personal experience, yet the experience of turning to God in conversion has its own indispensable role in the overall process."[29] Through Scripture, liturgy, hymnody and other means of grace, believers develop a framework of truth about God. This is essentially a process of shaping the mind into a Christian worldview that becomes the framework for recognizing and understanding personal encounter with God.

The means of grace also shape the affections. Maddox helps us to see that Wesley "assumed that acts of love would flow from a temper of love. Yet, he also recognized that ignorance, mistakes, and other human frailties often distort the passage from affection to action."[30] The means of grace contribute both to shaping holy tempers, and to character maturation, as all aspects of personhood are increasingly brought under the controlling principle of holy love. "Christian affections as emotions share particular qualities, and give direction to one's life as they are identified as one's character and virtues."[31] For Steele, since the affections are educated through the means of grace, "the church must take Christian formation seriously and provide the means for the education of the affections . . ."[32] The church facilitates growing knowledge of God by providing avenues for educating the affections as well as the mind.

These avenues form a network of influences through which believers develop desirable affections, or holy tempers. The interrelation of the affections, the means of grace and faith is the "key to understanding Christian growth."[33] Participation in the means of grace facilitates openness to the transforming power of the Holy Spirit. "The means of grace are by their very nature useful to God in forming affections and shaping tempers, because they convey God's identity and enable us to experience God's reality and to keep us focused on our neighbor."[34] The pursuit of holy habits, study of Scripture, prayer, service, are ways in which heart and mind take on the *habitus* of worship.

---

29. Abraham, "The Epistemology of Conversion," 189.

30. Maddox, "A Change of Affections," 21.

31. Steele, "Educating the Heart," 229.

32. Ibid., 231.

33. Knight, "The Role of Faith," 274.

34. Ibid., 283.

The means of grace are the practical measures through which the Wesleyan *ordo salutis* obtains existential meaning in ecclesial life. The knowledge of God is by faith, which grows through the means of grace. Orientation to fullness of communion implies that believers can expect to experience entire sanctification. Wesley asserts that "there is nothing more certain than that the Holy Spirit will not purify our nature, unless we carefully attend to his work in our lives."[35] He urges believers to go from faith to faith and to wait for entire sanctification by searching the Scriptures, partaking of the Lord's Supper, doing works of mercy, and continuing in fellowship with other believers. He insists that entire sanctification comes, "not without the means, but in the use of all those means which God has furnished."[36] Therefore, the use of the means of grace is the manner in which believers wait for entire sanctification.

Individuality and Fellowship

By making the quest for God the basis of unity and fellowship, and by integrating the experience of entire sanctification into ecclesial life, I have attempted to shed light on the theological and practical significance of holiness theology. The worshipful and inclusive ecclesial ethos generated by the quest for the knowledge of God is conducive to honoring the individual. Within the context of ecclesial fellowship, individuals can appropriate and exercise faith in unique ways with confidence of the community's respect and acceptance.

The life of faith is a deeply personal experience that varies from one individual to another. In addition, communion with God does not preclude challenges related to particular circumstances and individual emotional makeup or personality. A person's uniqueness and particular history influence the ability to express love. The ecclesial fellowship honors the individual by its acceptance of diversity in temperament, level of maturity and socio-ethnicity.

The ecclesial fellowship also honors individuals by respecting diversity in the ways individuals experience God. Variety in the form of religious experience is due to the complexity and uniqueness of individuals, as well as the freedom of divine action. "The various aspects of our humanity are all interrelated and inseparably interwoven into the

35. "On Grieving the Holy Spirit," *Works* VII: 489.
36. "On a Single Eye," *Works* VII: 299.

complex wholes that we are."[37] This complexity indicates that individual responses to the divine overture are not limited to a particular experiential paradigm. Some experiences of God may be "intense, focal, and of short duration" while others may be "non-focal, background, and long lasting."[38] The church demonstrates inclusiveness and mutual respect by acknowledging diversity in experience of God. Moreover, the circumstantial elements of religious experience have limited theological bearing on the teaching of entire sanctification. The communion model seeks to dissociate holiness theology from preoccupation with religious experience, not by negating personal experience of God, but by affirming that there are a variety of ways in which individuals experience God.

Accountability

In ecclesial fellowship, a balance of acceptance and accountability sustains worshipful character and orientation to fullness of communion. Accountability is a necessary element of genuine fellowship. The Holy Spirit establishes the church in the truth through its preaching and fellowship.

As the church lives in submission to the Holy Spirit, He guides the church in all truth. The Spirit convicts believers of truth and enables obedient response. Therefore, He holds the church accountable by His faithful activity and moves believers forward in the life of faith. In view of its assurance and continued expectation of the Spirit's activity, the church teaches and obeys Scripture in its corporate life, and encourages believers to walk in obedience. The church bears the responsibility of proclaiming biblical truth whereby the Spirit keeps the church holy and faithful.

The Wesleyan class meeting is a helpful pattern for developing groups of affirmation and accountability. Henderson argues that Wesley's class meeting system was "a powerful and effective educational method" for "nurturing and training Christian disciples."[39] These groups "met weekly to give an account of their personal spiritual growth."[40] These class meetings suggest a prototype for accountability through small group structures in present-day ecclesial communities. There were three guidelines for class meetings—do no harm, do all the good possible and attend

37. Mann, *Perfecting Grace*.

38. Alston, "The Autonomy of Religious Experience," 69.

39. Henderson, *A Model for Making Disciples*, 11.

40. Ibid., 11.

upon the means of grace. "By knowing the objective and the marks of growth, an individual and the community could observe and recognize progress in the journey of faith. A variety of structures were created to meet the needs of the journey, to nurture and sustain."[41] Groups of this type provide a safe space for individual patterns of confession, repentance, and accountability.[42]

Summation

This section has shown that the means of grace are necessary avenues for the Spirit's action in the church. Responsible and consistent use of the means of grace is a concrete expression of the church's quest for the knowledge of God. The means of grace facilitate the development of doxological character and orientation to fullness of communion. As the church thrives in its fellowship, it is empowered to participate in the divine mission.

Ecclesial Witness to Fullness of Communion

As the church hears and answers the call to fullness in the fellowship of holy love, it participates in the divine mission of extending redemptive fellowship. Through orientation to fullness of communion, the church becomes a fellowship of holy love with the power to form redemptive relationships and transcend the marginalization of persons. As the church expresses its fellowship with God through these evidences of genuine transformation, it witnesses to the reality of God's grace and its identity as the people of God.

The Fellowship of Holy Love

The pursuit of fullness of communion through the means of grace shapes the community of believers into a fellowship of holy love, through which it witnesses to the reality of Jesus Christ and becomes a means of grace to the world.

Humility is the essence of relationships that demonstrate participation in God. As discussed earlier, doxological ecclesial culture includes realization that the church lives by the grace of God alone and in complete

41. Matthaei, "Transcripts of the Trinity," 134.
42. Clapper, "Shaping Heart Religion," 220.

surrender to divine Lordship. Put differently, the doxological stance before God is one of humility. The paradigm for humility as an expression of holy love is the Son's *kenosis* (Phil 2:5–8). Thus, the church's participation in God results in relationships of self-giving. On this view, humility is the fundamental characteristic of the fellowship of holy love and the expression of the church's relation and likeness to Christ. In sum, through participation in God, Christian fellowship orients to the other—it is the fellowship of holy love.

This quality in Christian fellowship is the fundamental witness of the church that it belongs to the living Lord, because holy love is the evidence of the supernatural source of the church's being. Holy love is the particularity of the people of God since it is only in relation to Christ through the Holy Spirit that relationships can take on the character of humility. Relationships of holy love differentiate the community of believers from social groups arising on any other basis besides Jesus Christ. The church can be a fellowship of holy love only because its fellowship is in Christ. Accordingly, the church witnesses to the reality of Jesus Christ to the extent that it is this kind of fellowship.

Since the capacity for mutual self-giving is definitive of the church of Jesus Christ, it is this uniqueness that constitutes the authentic basis for seeking others for fellowship. First, one dimension of self-giving is the free overture to the other for fellowship. As such, the community of believers experiences the compulsion of holy love to joyfully seek out and invite others into fellowship. Second, this overture is free. As the fellowship of holy love, the church reaches out for the sake of fellowship. In doing this, the church is only expressing its participation in the self-giving God. Finally, this kind of outreach distinguishes the church from organizations of human origin. It points to the church's uniqueness in the world, as the community in which persons can know unconditional love. Demonstrations of unconditional love disclose the church's function as God's means of grace in the world, and only in this demonstration does the church fulfill its function as means of grace.

To conclude, the community of faith, to the extent that it models holy love, is the means by which God draws unbelievers into fellowship with Himself. By the unity and power of its fellowship in the Spirit, the church is a visible sacrament. Through its unconditional self-giving, the church incarnates grace to the world. The church functions as a means of grace by maintaining its doxological character and orientation to communion with God, which is the wellspring that nourishes ecclesial power to love. The church is a means of grace only as it continually experiences the Spirit's transformative grace, comforting love, and illuminating wisdom.

Redemptive Action

Unconditional love is the source of redemption. Therefore, through its self-giving, the church establishes redemptive relationships and in this way, it is the channel through which God enacts His salvific mission. On this view, the mission of the church is to act redemptively in the world as the expression of its participation in God.

Redemptive relationships are those through which the Spirit works to transform the lives, the vision, and the situation of persons. The church is commissioned and empowered to enact this redemption. Thus, "the love we have from God reaches out to others, forging the bonds of grace linking us to one another in a community of love that encompasses us all. To be a Christian in the world is to be an instrument of God helping to forge the God-intended community of love and justice."[43] Ecclesial fellowship in the Spirit shapes believers in the capacity to act redemptively. The church can and must do this because its source of power is divine grace. As the church, grounded in divine grace, thrives in worship, submission, and allegiance, it can act redemptively.

Unconditional love goes out to meet the other in situations that need redemption. This amounts to purposeful, costly self-giving. Therefore, the church gives its mission concrete form by becoming an agent of change. This entails reaching into unfamiliar contexts. It means that the church develops action plans to put its resources to use in ways that may bring no return. Redemptive action is needed precisely where there is no love, gratitude or openness to grace. It is action in places of human despair and degradation. The cross of Jesus Christ witnesses to the cost of redemptive action. However, it also witnesses to the power of redemptive action. Therefore, the church's self-outpouring is authorized and empowered because in this self-outpouring, the church demonstrates its union with Christ and His mission.

The church carries out this mission by using its resources to signal its character as a community of hope in which people "experience the power and presence of God's love."[44] This calls for programs and outreach

43. Wogaman, "The Doctrine of God and Dilemmas of Power," 37.
44. Heitzenrater, "Wesleyan Ecclesiology," 127.

ministries aimed at giving hope. As Joy suggests, a congregation may evaluate its commitment to redemptive action by asking these questions:

> In our evangelization and educational outreach ministries, are we canvassing the whole populations around us? What proportions of our energy and resources are spent on maintenance of our own program? What proportion on the work of God beyond our community? What feelings are evoked in persons among us who experience unemployment, illegitimate pregnancy, divorce, or other tragedies or sensations of failure?"[45]

Such questions point the church to situations that are in need of redemption, and indicate the extent to which it engages in redemptive action.

Transcending Marginalization

Marginalized persons are those who have reason to question their acceptance by the majority of society. When the church orients to fullness of communion, it has the power to transcend marginalization by refusing to acknowledge the categorization of persons along the lines of an ungodly world order. The Wesleyan-Holiness tradition has a history of identifying with the marginalized, which provides insight for the contemporary situation.

The church expresses its participation in Christ and His mission by refusing to approach others in terms of non-biblical criteria of personal identity. Put differently, the church refuses to accept the marginalization of persons. Inclusiveness is one way that the church demonstrates that it lives in the expectation and experience of fullness of communion. Living in submission to the Holy Spirit, the church has divine light to see beyond socio-cultural categorization of persons. The church under divine Lordship can and must choose to see persons in divine light (Ps 36:9). The church that operates in harmony with its participation in God values persons because they are loved by God. As Wolterstorff argues, "God loves each and every human being equally and permanently" and this is the basis for the worth of persons.[46] This view gives the church a theological rationale for breaking through socio-economic and ethnic barriers. By virtue of its counter-cultural conception of persons, the church is itself a marginalized community. The church fully embraces its character as a doxological community of holy

45. Joy, "The Contemporary Church," 406.
46. Wolterstorff, *Justice: Rights and Wrongs*, 360.

fellowship by rejoicing in its marginalization. In this stance, the church is glad to be in the world, but "not of the world" (John 17:16), and as such, is able to overcome the world (1 John 5:4–5).

Scripture provides principles by which to transcend marginalization. First, oneness in Christ takes priority over socio-economic status, race and gender (Gal 3:28). While these distinctions are sociological realities, they do not constitute the ground of the church's engagement with people. Instead, the church's approach is conditioned by its conviction of the intrinsic worth of persons. This counter-cultural stance is not for the sake of social justice. Rather, it is for the sake of genuine oneness in Christ—oneness created by, in and through the fellowship and lordship of the Holy Spirit. Second, allegiance to Jesus Christ includes adopting His approach to people, as demonstrated in the Gospel story. In His relationships He embraced the marginalized (Matt 9:10). He included them in His circle of acceptance. He affirmed the value of the poor, oppressed masses of Palestine to their heavenly Father (Matt 10:31). He expressed the worth of persons by sharing Himself, conversing with them, feeding them, and healing them (Matt 11:5). In sum, Jesus develops authentic relationships with the marginalized. His compassion takes visible, transformative from. His love takes the form of patience and self-giving. Moreover, one senses that Jesus likes the poor of Palestine. When the church chooses to approach others from this standpoint, it participates in the divine mission, and, over time, this becomes a part of its identity. The realization of fullness of communion imparts the requisite transformation that allows the church to do this.

The Wesleyan-Holiness tradition has a history of solidarity with the marginalized, in the form of compassion for the poor. Dayton demonstrates this commitment in Wesley's life-style.[47] Founding leaders of the tradition brought this solidarity into the twentieth century. As Dayton shows, B. T. Roberts, founder of the Free Methodist denomination, considered this commitment to be definitive of the true church.[48] For Roberts, the biblical rationale for ministering to the poor was the testimony of Jesus to John the Baptist that the poor have the gospel preached to them.[49] Phineas Bresee urged the newly organized Church of the Nazarene to minister to the poor as a witness to its union with Christ. He states, "when on earth, Jesus

47. Dayton, "The Wesleyan Option for the Poor," 10.

48. Ibid., 14.

49. Ibid.

declared the crowning evidence of His divine mission to be that 'the poor have the gospel preached to them'; so today the evidence of the presence of Jesus in our midst is that we bear the gospel, primarily, to the poor."[50] Moreover, the fact that a beggar was the recipient of the first miracle after Pentecost means, for Bresee, that the baptism with the Holy Spirit requires ministry to the poor.[51] As the Wesleyan-Holiness tradition seeks to live in resonance with its founding principles, it must do so with sensitivity to the present context in which marginalization extends beyond socio-economic status to include gender, ethnicity and religion. The present global situation of mass disenfranchisement of persons presents the church with a critical imperative to develop structures that overcome a range of injustices.

The church transcends marginalization because of the intrinsic worth of all persons. On this basis, it follows the example of Jesus. Joy suggests that, like Jesus, the church must become poor.[52] The church, as the body of Christ, is called to enact "becoming poor" by taking up the cause of the wronged, "to become the advocate and the defender of the abused and the humiliated."[53] By entering into the space of the marginalized, believers share in human suffering. This participation, even when it does not change a social situation, expresses genuine interest in persons. That is to say, the church affirms the value of individuals by communicating the desire for genuine fellowship.

Becoming poor is not merely becoming a benefactor of the underprivileged. Instead, it is affirming that the other has a story to share.[54] Put differently, transcending marginalization means honoring the disenfranchised as persons with whom the church must engage in genuine reciprocity—acceptance, respect, and friendship. In this dual movement of reaching outward and drawing in, the church acknowledges the intrinsic value of *all* persons. This movement is itself counter-cultural because it refuses to recognize the social and economic categorization of persons. In doing this, the church continually calls upon God for divine wisdom in carrying out its God-given mission. Thus, from first to last, the church must live in submission to the Holy Spirit. It is the case that these guidelines describe an ideal that is most of the time far from the

---

50. Bresee, "The Prince of Life."

51. Ibid.

52. Joy, "The Contemporary Church," 427.

53. Ibid., 428.

54. Johnson, "Remembering the Poor," 196.

reality. Nonetheless, fullness of communion suggests that this the church can and must participate in the divine overture to all persons. At bottom, the ecclesial significance of holiness theology is made visible through expressions of holy love, which testify to the reality of divine grace in a hurting world.

Summation

The church witnesses to its union with Christ by its fellowship of unconditional, sacrificial love. The quality of ecclesial fellowship reflects fullness in its relationship with God. Unconditional love compels the church to act redemptively in the world. This is its mission as the Body of Christ. Furthermore, in its redemptive action, the church breaks down marginalization by entering into the situation of marginalization, and by approaching persons in terms of their identity as those loved by God.

Conclusion

This chapter has shown the ecclesial significance of holiness theology in the communion paradigm. First, holiness theology obtains significance by orienting ecclesial life to fullness of communion. The church seeks the knowledge of God in submission, adoration and allegiance, which are doxological attitudes. Thus, the church lives out its single quest for the knowledge of God in and through a doxological stance whereby it is drawn into fullness of communion.

In this posture, the church understands its public worship to be the occasion of divine-human encounter, the mutual enjoyment of creaturely presence before God, and divine presence to the church through the Holy Spirit. Creaturely enjoyment of God takes the form of glorifying God, and as God is glorified in His church, He sanctifies His people. Therefore, the church lives in the expectation that in worship, believers are drawn into deeper fellowship, and may receive the grace of entire sanctification. The nurture of doxological character is the matrix in which the church advances in the knowledge of God.

Based on the biblical account of the primitive church, the doxological stance is the privilege of all believers, and is not limited to the Wesleyan-Holiness tradition. Thus, in its orientation to fullness of communion, the tradition stands on common ground with Christian tradition as a whole, which allows it to voice its distinctive understanding of divine-human fellowship, and to hear the voices of other traditions in this regard. Within the tradition itself, holiness theology in the communion paradigm underwrites ecclesial life. By directing ecclesial focus to the knowledge of God, believers are joined by their common quest. Consistent pursuit of the knowledge of God brings believers into entire sanctification and fullness of communion.

Second, the means of grace nurture doxological character. Use of the ordained and prudential means of grace shapes believers in the truth, both cognitively and affectively. The church facilitates the use of the means of grace in faith that the Holy Spirit will, by these means, draw believers into closer fellowship with God and one another. Sensitivity to individuality and contextual relevance and the need for accountability are principles that come into play in developing the form of the means of grace in the fellowship of believers.

Finally, the church expresses its orientation to fullness of communion through its witness as a fellowship of holy love. To the extent that holiness and love mark ecclesial fellowship, the church witnesses to the reality of divine grace and fellowship with God. The church demonstrates its connection to God by its capacity for unconditional love, expressed through concrete actions of self-giving to draw persons into redemptive relationships. The church demonstrates its power by its capacity to draw unbelievers into meaningful relationships through the affirmation of the value of the individual. This decisiveness brings the church to the culmination of its expression of solidarity with God: solidarity with the marginalized. Without fear, and in the power of the Holy Spirit, the church is called to enter into the space of the marginalized and to transcend social categorization of persons. It does this by ascribing value to persons because of their value to God. As the church moves outward, its inclusive attitude opens the way for the marginalized to share in ecclesial fellowship.

6

Conclusion

THE AIM OF THIS project has been to map out and apply a new paradigm for holiness theology. The need for the project was established by identifying a strand of anthropocentrism in current holiness theology. Theological reflection from the starting point of personal experience has resulted in over-valuing the human role in religious experience and overshadowing the primacy of grace. It has also led to a reduction in the scope of holiness theology to the sphere of moral theology.

Chapter 2 identified Wesley's dynamic *ordo salutis* as the framework for his teaching on Christian perfection and demonstrated the reduction of this teaching to the single crisis of entire sanctification in the early days of the American Holiness Movement. The key issue in this paradigm shift was the revision in concept of faith, which contributed to the move from experiential to self-referential holiness theology.

Chapter 3 traced the relation of participation in God and holiness theology in the thought of John Wesley and Phineas Bresee. The transcendent goal of entire sanctification was shown to be fullness in divine-human fellowship. This provided the standpoint for developing the parameters of a communion paradigm. When approached from the perspective of communion with God, the root of holiness theology is the triune fellowship of holy love and its context is the dynamic *ordo salutis* of increasing participation in God. On this view, entire sanctification is an element of a crisis-process interaction of genuine divine-human reciprocity. As such, holiness theology attests to the preeminence of grace, and moral responsibility as an enablement of grace. Holiness is the outcome of participation in God rather than the goal of entire sanctification.

On this basis, chapter 4 explicated the dynamics of entire sanctification. The proposed thesis was that in entire sanctification, divine-human fellowship reaches a decisive moment of faith in which the Holy Spirit cleanses away inherited sin and establishes fullness of communion. Sin, a pervasive principle of idolatry and unbelief, was shown to be antithetical to the knowledge of God and the lordship of Jesus Christ. Through the Spirit's enablement, believers are brought to a decisive moment of repentance and faith for entire sanctification. In this experience, the Holy Spirit assumes control of the believer's heart, and holy love becomes the ruling principle of human existence. This new quality of fellowship is evidenced by a greater capacity to flourish in the fruit of the Spirit.

Chapter 5 discussed the ecclesial implications of orientation to fullness of communion. A common quest for the knowledge of God shapes the church in doxological character. Orientation to fullness of communion is practically carried out by faithfully providing and encouraging the use of the means of grace. This is the locus of an ecclesial fellowship that respects individuality and exercises responsible accountability. Finally, the church expresses its orientation to fullness of communion through its witness. The primary act of witnessing is the church's power for sacrificial, unconditional love. This capacity to love is the sign of the reality of divine-human fellowship and transformative grace. The church demonstrates its power by its redemptive action and counter-cultural stance in affirming that God's love ascribes intrinsic value to persons. On this basis, the church embraces and dissolves marginalization. Its identification with the disenfranchised is based upon its life in God and its sure knowledge that divine holiness and love, through the presence and action of the Holy Spirit breathes love, redemption and inclusiveness into situations of despair. The communion paradigm suggests these concrete ways in which holiness doctrine shapes ecclesial culture and life.

The communion paradigm offers a possible way out of the present impasse in holiness theology. Further reflection would serve to elucidate the connection of holiness theology to the wider theological system with greater detail and precision. Faith, understood as participatory knowledge of God, can function as a methodological key in developing theologies of Trinity and church. This is a valid methodological approach because the concept of the knowledge of faith points to divine revelation and life, as well as the divine salvific mission. Revelation and mission fuse together in the affirmation of the Spirit's presence as the cause and life of the church.

The central Wesleyan theme of heart religion suggests personal actualization of the grand themes of systematic theology. Yet, the locus of this actualization, the personal experience of the believer, is not the necessary, nor the desired starting point of reflection. The motivation for this project has been to articulate an experiential Wesleyan-Holiness theology that does not begin with personal experience. This is not to negate anthropology. In fact, the communion paradigm can be further clarified and strengthened if accompanied by a robust theological anthropology.

The communion paradigm provides the theological foundation for a practical theology. Practitioners in spiritual formation and Christian education can use the knowledge of God, or heart religion, as an integrative theme to orient small group and other educational structures. The paradigm provides a theological rationale for engagement in issues of social justice. It thus provides a rudimentary ground for the development of a Wesleyan moral theology.

Finally, this book has sought to establish a single precept—the doctrine of holiness attests to divine holiness and its out-flow of holy love, as it has been revealed through our Lord Jesus Christ, and continues to be revealed by the Holy Spirit in the Church. Personal transformation and authentic ecclesial fellowship are signs pointing back to the divine life.

Bibliography

Abraham, William J. "The Epistemology of Conversion: Is There Something New?" In *Conversion in the Wesleyan Tradition*, edited by Kenneth J. Collins and John H. Tyson, 175–94. Nashville: Abingdon, 2001.

Agnew, Milton S. "Baptized with the Spirit." *Wesleyan Theological Journal* 14.1 (1979) 7–14.

Alston, William P. "The Autonomy of Religious Experience." *International Journal for Philosophy of Religion* 31.2–3 (1992) 67–87.

Arnett, William M. "The Role of the Holy Spirit in Entire Sanctification in the Writings of John Wesley." *Wesleyan Theological Journal* 14.2 (1979) 15–30.

Augello, Joseph Lawrence, Jr. "The American Wesleyan-Holiness Movement's Doctrine of Entire Sanctification: A Reformulation." Ph. D. diss., The Southern Baptist Theological Seminary, 2003.

Ayers, Jeremy. "John Wesley's Therapeutic Understanding of Salvation." *Encounter* 63.2 (2002) 263–97.

Bassett, Paul Merritt. "A Study in the Theology of the Early Holiness Movement." *Methodist History* 13.3 (1975) 61–84.

———. "The Interplay of Christology and Ecclesiology in the Theology of the Holiness Movement." *Wesleyan Theological Journal* 16.2 (1981) 79–94.

———. "The Theological Identity of the North American Holiness Movement." In *The Variety of American Evangelicalism*, edited by Donald W. Dayton and Robert K. Johnston, 72–108. Knoxville, TN: University of Tennessee Press, 1991.

Berg, Daniel N. "The Theological Context of American Wesleyanism." *Wesleyan Theological Journal* 20.1 (1985) 45–60.

Bolster, George R. "Wesley's Doctrine of Justification." *Evangelical Quarterly* 24 (1952) 144–55.

Brantley, Richard E. *Locke, Wesley, and the Method of English Romanticism*. Gainesville, FL: University of Florida Press, 1984.

Bresee, Phineas. *The Certainties of Faith*. Kansas City, MO: Nazarene, 1958. No pages. Online: http://wesley.nnu.edu/wesleyctr/books/2501-2600/HDM2579.pdf.

———. *Twenty-Nine Sermons* Abridged ed. Los Angeles, CA: Nazarene, 1903; Digital Edition 05/19/96 by Holiness Data Ministry 1903. No pages. Online: http://wesley.nnu.edu/wesleyctr/books/0101-0200/HDM0192.pdf.

Brindlinger, Irv A. "Transformative Dimensions within Wesley's Understanding of Christian Perfection." *Asbury Theological Journal* 59.1–2 (2004) 117–26.

Carver, Frank G. "Biblical Foundations for the 'Secondness' of Entire Sanctification." *Wesleyan Theological Journal* 22.2 (1987) 7–23.

Charry, Ellen T. "The Soteriological Importance of the Divine Perfections." In *God the Holy Trinity: Reflections on Christian Faith and Practice*, edited by Timothy George, 129–47. Grand Rapids: Baker Academic, 2006.

Christensen, Michael J. "John Wesley: Christian Perfection as Faith Filled with the Energy of Love." In *Partakers of the Divine Nature: The History and Development of Deification*, edited by Michael J. Christensen and Jeffery A. Wittung, 219–27. Grand Rapids: Baker Academic, 2008.

Clapper, Gregory S. "Shaping Heart Religion through Preaching and Pastoral Care." In *"Heart Religion" in the Methodist Tradition and Related Movements*, edited by Richard B. Steele, 209–24. Lanham, MD: Scarecrow, 2001.

Collins, Kenneth J. "A Hermeneutical Model for the Wesleyan Ordo Salutis." *Wesleyan Theological Journal* 19.2 (1984) 23–37.

———. "John Wesley's Topography of the Heart: Dispostions, Tempers, and Affections." *Methodist History* 36.3 (1998) 162–75.

———. "Recent Trends in Wesleyan-Holiness Scholarship." *Wesleyan Theological Journal* 35.1 (2000) 67–86.

———. *The Theology of John Wesley: Holy Love and the Shape of Grace*. Nashville: Abingdon, 2007.

Colón-Emeric, Edgardo Antonio. *Perfection in Dialogue: An Ecumenical Encounter between Wesley and Aquinas*. Waco, TX: Baylor University Press, 2007.

Colyer, Elmer M., and Corrie M. Aukema Cieslukowski. "Wesley's Trinitarian Ordo Salutis." *Reformation & Revival* 14.4 (2005) 105–31.

Coppedge, Allan. "Entire Sanctification in Early American Methodism: 1812–1835." *Wesleyan Theological Journal* 13 (1978) 34–50.

Cox, Leo G. *John Wesley's Concept of Perfection*. Kansas City, MO: Beacon Hill, 1964.

———. "Prevenient Grace: A Wesleyan View." Journal of the Evangelical Theological Society 12.3 (1969) 143-149.

Dayton, Donald. "Asa Mahan and the Development of Holiness Theology." *Wesleyan Theological Journal* 9, no. 1 (1974): 60-69.

———. "Presidential Address: The Wesleyan Option for the Poor." *Wesleyan Theological Journal* 26 (1991) 7–22.

Deasley, Alex R. G. "The Church in the Acts of the Apostles." In *The Church: An Inquiry into Ecclesiology from a Biblical Theological Perspective*, edited by Daniel N. Berg and Melvin E. Dieter, 47–88. Anderson, IN: Warner, 1984.

———. "Entire Sanctification and the Baptism with the Holy Spirit: Perspectives on the Biblical View of the Relationship." *Wesleyan Theological Journal* 14.1 (1979) 27–44.

Dieter, Melvin. "The Development of Nineteenth-Century Holiness Theology." *Wesleyan Theological Journal* 20.1 (1985) 61–77.

———. *The Holiness Revival of the Nineteenth Century*. 2nd ed. Studies in Evangelicalism. Lanham, MD: Scarecrow, 1996.

Dieter, Melvin, and Daniel Berg, editors. *The Church: An Inquiry into Ecclesiology from a Biblical Theological Persepctive*. Anderson, IN: Warner, 1984.

Dorr, Donal J. "Wesley's Teaching on the Nature of Holiness." *London Quarterly and Holborn Review* 190 (1965) 234–39.

Dreyer, Frederick. "Faith and Experience in the Thought of John Wesley." *The American Historical Review* 88.1 (1983) 12–30.

Dunning, H. Ray. "Christian Perfection: Toward a New Paradigm." *Wesleyan Theological Journal* 33.1 (1998) 151–63.

————. *Grace, Faith and Holiness: A Wesleyan Systematic Theology.* Kansas City, MO: Beacon Hill, 1988

Easley, Kendell H. "The Pauline Usage of Pneumati as a Reference to the Spirit of God." *Journal of the Evangelical Theological Society* 27.3 (1984) 299–313.

Fletcher, John. *The Works of the Rev. John Fletcher with a Life by the Rev. Abraham Scott.* 2 Vols. London: Allman, 1836.

Flew, R. Newton. *The Idea of Perfection in Christian Theology: An Historical Study of the Christian Ideal for the Present Life.* New York: Humanities, 1968.

George, Paul R. Jr. "Selfhood and the Search for an Identity: Explaining the Emergence of the Nineteenth-Century Holiness Movement and Early Church of the Nazarene." Ph.D. diss., Western Michigan University, 2004.

Goroncy, Jason. "The Elusiveness, Loss and Cruciality of Recovered Holiness: Some Biblical and Theological Observations." *International Journal of Systematic Theology* 10.2 (2008) 195–209.

Grabowski, John S. "Person: Substance and Relation." *Communio* 22 (1995) 139–63.

Grenz, Stanley J. *The Social God and the Relational Self.* Louisville, KY: Westminster John Knox, 2002.

Greathouse, William M., and Paul Bassett. *Exploring Christian Holiness. Vol. 2. The Historical Development.* Kansas City, MO: Beacon Hill, 1985.

Greathouse, William M., and George Lyons. *Romans 1–8: A Commentary in the Wesleyan Tradition.* New Beacon Bible Commentary. Kansas City, MO: Beacon Hill, 2008.

Gregory the Great. *Homilia in Evangelium* 27.4. In *Patrologia Latina*, vol. 76, edited by J. -P. Migne, 1207. 217 vols. Paris: Migne, 1844–64.

Grider, J. Kenneth. "Spirit Baptism the Means of Sanctification: A Response to the Lyon View." *Wesleyan Theological Journal* 14.2 (1979) 31–50.

————. *A Wesleyan-Holiness Theology.* Kansas City, MO: Beacon Hill, 1994

Heitzenrater, Richard P. "God with Us: Grace and the Spiritual Senses in John Wesley's Theology." In *Grace upon Grace: Essays in Honor of Thomas A. Langford*, edited by Robert K. Johnston, L. Gregory Jones and Jonathan R. Wilson, 87–109. Nashville: Abingdon, 1999.

————. "Wesleyan Ecclesiology: Methodism as a Means of Grace." In *Orthodox and Wesleyan Ecclesiology*, edited by S. T. Kimbrough, Jr., 119–28. New York: St. Vladimir's Seminary Press, 2007.

Henderson, D. Michael. *A Model for Making Disciples: John Wesley's Class Meeting.* Nappanee, IN: Evangel, 1997.

Hynson, Leon O. "The Wesleyan Quadrilateral in the American Holiness Tradition." *Wesleyan Theological Journal* 20.1 (1985) 19–33.

Ingersol, Stan. *Nazarene Roots: Pastors, Prophets, Revivalists & Reformers.* Kansas City, MO: Beacon Hill, 2009.

Johnson, J. Prescott. "Crisis and Con-Sequence: Sanctification and the Greek Tense." *Wesleyan Theological Journal* 37.2 (2002) 172-93.

Johnson, Susanne. "Remembering the Poor: Transforming Christian Practice." In *Redemptive Transformation in Practical Theology: Essays in Honor of James E. Loder Jr.*, edited by Dana R. Wright & John D. Kuentzel, 189–215. Grand Rapids: Eerdmans, 2004.

Johnson, W. Stanley. "Christian Perfection as Love for God." *Wesleyan Theological Journal* 18.1 (1983) 50–60.

Bibliography

Joy, Donald M. "The Contemporary Church as 'Holy Community': Call to Corporate Character and Life." In *The Church: An Inquiry into Ecclesiology from a Biblical Theological Perspective*, edited by Daniel N. Berg and Melvin E. Dieter, 397–432. Anderson, IN: Warner, 1984.

Knight, Henry H. III. "Love and Freedom 'by Grace Alone' in Wesley's Soteriology: A Proposal for Evangelicals." *Pneuma* 24.1 (2002) 57–67.

———. *The Presence of God in the Christian Life: John Wesley and the Means of Grace.* Metuchen, NJ: Scarecrow, 1992.

———. "The Role of Faith and the Means of Grace in the Heart Religion of John Wesley." In *"Heart Religion" in the Methodist Tradition and Related Movements*, edited by Richard B. Steele, 273–90. Lanham, MD: Scarecrow, 2001.

———. "The Transformation of the Human Heart: The Place of Conversion in Wesley's Theology." In *Conversion in the Wesleyan Tradition*, edited by Kenneth J. Collins and John H. Tyson, 43–55. Nashville: Abingdon, 2001.

———. "Worship and Sanctification." *Wesleyan Theological Journal* 32.2 (1997) 5–14.

Knight, John A. "John Fletcher's Influence on the Development of Wesleyan Theology in America." *Wesleyan Theological Journal* 13 (1978) 13–33.

Küschner, Mathias J. "The Enthusiasm of the Rev. John Wesley." *Wesleyan Theological Journal* 35.2 (2000) 114–37.

Leclerc, Diane. *Discovering Christian Holiness: The Heart of Wesleyan-Holiness Theology.* Kansas City, MO: Beacon Hill, 2010.

———. "Phoebe Palmer: Spreading 'Accessible' Holiness." In *From Aldersgate to Azusa Street*, 90–98. Eugene, OR: Pickwick, 2010.

Lowery, Kevin T. "A Fork in the Wesleyan Road: Phoebe Palmer and the Appropriation of Christian Perfection." *Wesleyan Theological Journal* 36.2 (2001) 187–222.

Lyon, Robert W. "Baptism and Spirit-Baptism in the New Testament." *Wesleyan Theological Journal* 14.1 (1979) 14–26.

Maddox, Randy L. "A Change of Affections: The Development, Dynamics, and Dethronement of John Wesley's Heart Religion." In *"Heart Religion" in the Methodist Tradition and Related Movements*, edited by Richard B. Steele, 3–31. Lanham, MD: Scarecrow, 2001.

———. *Responsible Grace: John Wesley's Practical Theology.* Nashville: Kingswood, 1994.

Mann, Mark H. *Perfecting Grace: Holiness, Human Being and the Sciences.* New York, London: T. & T. Clark, 2006.

Mannoia, Kevin W., and Don Thorsen, editors. *The Holiness Manifesto.* Grand Rapids: Eerdmans, 2008.

Matthaei, Sondra. "Transcripts of the Trinity: Communion and Community in Formation for Holiness of Heart and Life." *Quarterly Review* 18.2 (1998) 123–37.

Matthews, Rex D. "'With the Eyes of Faith': Spiritual Experience and the Knowledge of God in the Theology of John Wesley." In *Wesleyan Theology Today: A Bicentennial Consultation*, edited by Theodore Runyan, 406–15. Nashville, TN: Kingswood, 1985.

McGonigle, Herbert Boyd. *Sufficient Saving Grace: John Wesley's Evangelical Arminianism.* Paternoster Biblical and Theological Monographs. Carlisle, UK: Paternoster, 2001.

Meeks, Douglas M. "Trinity, Community, and Power." In *Trinity, Community, and Power: Mapping Trajectories in Wesleyan Theology*, edited by Douglas M. Meeks, 15–31. Nashville: Kingswood, 2000.

Miles, Rebekah. "'The Arts of Holy Living': Holiness and the Means of Grace." *Quarterly Review* 25.2 (2005) 141–57.

Mitchell, T. Crichton, editor. *The Wesley Century (1725–1825)*. Great Holiness Classics, Vol. 2. Kansas City, MO: Beacon Hill, 1984.

Moberly, R. W. L. "'Holy, Holy, Holy': Isaiah's Vision of God." In *Holiness Past and Present*, edited by Stephen C. Barton, 122–40. London: T. & T. Clark, 2003.

Neff, Blake J. "John Wesley and John Fletcher on Entire Sanctificaiton: A Metaphoric Cluster Analysis." Ph.D. diss., Bowling Green State Universtiy, 1982.

Noble, T. A. "John Wesley as a Theologian: An Introduction." *Evangelical Quarterly* 82.3 (2010) 238–57.

Oord, Thomas J. "Attaining Perfection: Love for God and Neighbor." In *Spiritual Formation: A Wesleyan Perspective*, edited by Diane Leclerc and Mark A. Maddix, 65–73. Kansas City, MO: Beacon Hill, 2011.

Outler, Albert Cook, and Richard P. Heitzenrater, editors. *John Wesley's Sermons: An Anthology*. Nashville: Abingdon, 1991.

Palmer, Phoebe. *The Way of Holiness, with Notes by the Way: Being a Narrative of Religious Experience Resulting from a Determination to Be a Bible Christian*. London: Nichols, 1856.

Peters, John L. *Christian Perfection and American Methodism*. New York: Abingdon, 1956.

Powell, Samuel M. "The Theological Significance of the Holiness Movement" *Quarterly Review* 25.2 (2005) 126–40.

Quanstrom, Mark R. *A Century of Holiness Theology: The Doctrine of Entire Sanctification in the Church of the Nazarene: 1905 to 2004*. Kansas City, MO: Beacon Hill, 2004.

Rakestraw, Robert V. "John Wesley as a Theologian of Grace." *Journal of the Evangelical Theological Society* 27.2 (1984) 193–203.

Reasoner, Victor Paul. "The American Holiness Movement's Paradigm Shift Concerning Pentecost." *Wesleyan Theological Journal* 31.2 (1996) 132–46.

Robertson, A. T. *Robertson's Word Pictures of the New Testament* (1960). Online: *Bible Study Tools*. http://www.biblestudytools.com/commentaries/robertsons-word-pictures (accessed December 2010).

Schlimm, Matthew R. "The Puzzle of Perfection: Growth in John Wesley's Doctrine of Perfection." *Wesleyan Theological Journal* 38.2 (2003) 124–42.

Schneider, A. Gregory. "A Conflict of Associations: The National Camp-Meeting Association for the Promotion of Holiness Versus the Methodist Episcopal Church." *Church History* 66.2 (1997) 268–83.

Smith, Timothy L. *Called Unto Holiness*. Vol. 2. Kansas City, MO: Nazarene, 1962.

———. "A Chronological List of Wesley's Sermons and Doctrinal Essays." *Wesleyan Theological Journal* 17.2 (1982) 88–110.

———. "John Wesley and the Second Blessing." *Wesleyan Theological Journal* 21.1–2 (1986) 137–58.

Staples, Rob L. "John Wesley's Doctrine of the Holy Spirit." *Wesleyan Theological Journal* 21.1–2 (1986) 91–115.

Steele, Les L. "Educating the Heart." In *"Heart Religion" in the Methodist Tradition and Related Movements*, edited by Richard B. Steele, 225–44. Lanham, MD: Scarecrow, 2001.

Taylor, Richard S. *Exploring Christian Holiness. Vol. 3. The Theological Formulation.* Kansas City, MO: Beacon Hill, 1985.

———, editor. *Leading Wesleyan Thinkers.* Great Holiness Classics, Vol. 3. Kansas City, MO: Beacon Hill, 1985.

Taylor, Richard S., W. T. Purkiser, and Willard H. Taylor. *God, Man and Salvation.* Kansas City, MO: Beacon Hill, 1977.

Thobaben, James R. "Holy Knowing: A Wesleyan Epistemology." In *The Death of Metaphysics; the Death of Culture: Epistemology, Metaphysics, and Morality*, edited by Mark J. Cherry, 99–132. Dordrecht: Springer, 2006.

Turner, George Allen. "The Baptism of the Holy Spirit in the Wesleyan Tradition." *Wesleyan Theological Journal* 14.1 (1979) 60–76.

———. *The Vision Which Transforms.* Kansas City, MO: Beacon Hill, 1964.

Wainwright, Geoffrey. *Doxology: The Praise of God in Worship, Doctrine and Life.* New York: Oxford University Press, 1980.

Webster, John. "The Holiness and Love of God." *Scottish Journal of Theology* 57.3 (2004) 249–68.

Wesley, John. *The Bicentennial Edition of the Works of John Wesley.* General editors, Frank Baker and Richard P. Heitzenrater. Nashville: Abingdon, 1976–.

———. *Explanatory Notes Upon the New Testament.* New York: Lane & Scott, 1850.

———. *The Works of John Wesley.* 14 vols. 3rd ed. Kansas City, MO: Beacon Hill, 1979.

White, Charles Edward. "Phoebe Palmer and the Development of Pentecostal Pneumatology." *Wesleyan Theological Journal* 23.1–2 (1988) 198–212.

Wiley, H. Orton. *Christian Theology.* 3 vols. Kansas City, MO: Beacon Hill, 1940.

Williams, Colin W. *John Wesley's Theology Today.* New York: Abingdon, 1960.

Wogaman, J. Philip. "The Doctrine of God and Dilemmas of Power." In *Trinity, Community, and Power: Mapping Trajectories in Wesleyan Theology*, edited by Douglas M. Meeks, 33–50. Nashville: Kingswood, 2000.

Wolterstorff, Nicholas. *Justice: Rights and Wrongs.* Princeton: Princeton University Press, 2008.

Wood, Charles M. "Methodist Doctrine: An Understanding." *Quarterly Review* 22.3 (1998) 167–82.

Wood, L. W. "Exegetical-Theological Reflections on the Baptism with the Holy Spirit." *Wesleyan Theological Journal* 14.2 (1979) 51–63.

———. *The Meaning of Pentecost in Early Methodism: Rediscovering John Fletcher as John Wesley's Vindicator and Designated Successor.* Pietist and Wesleyan Studies 15. Lanham, MD: Scarecrow, 2002.

———. *Pentecostal Grace.* Grand Rapids: Francis Asbury, 1980.

———. "Pentecostal Sanctification in Wesley and Early Methodism." *Pneuma* 21.2 (1999) 251–87.

———. "Wesley's Epistemology." *Wesleyan Theological Journal* 10 (1975) 48–59.

Wood, Susan K. "The Liturgy." In *Knowing the Triune God: The Work of the Spirit in the Practices of the Church*, edited by James J. Buckley and David S. Yeago, 95–118. Grand Rapids: Eerdmans, 2001.

Wynkoop, Mildred Bangs. *A Theology of Love.* Kansas City, MO: Beacon Hill, 1972.

———. "Theological Roots of Wesleyanism's Understanding of the Holy Spirit." *Wesleyan Theological Journal* 14.1 (1979) 77–98.